PT Boat 81
Still On WW II Nightmare Patrol

Rev 23 August 2023

Narrated by Milt Rackham
Written by Myrl Thompson

Paperback ISBN: 978-1-648-734-113
Hardback ISBN: 978-1-64873-416-8
Ebook: ISBN: 978-1-64873-417-5
LCCN - 2023917518

Copyright © 2023 Myrl Thompson

Printed in the United States of America

**Published by: Writer's Publishing House
Prescott, AZ 86301**

Cover Design, Project Management, and Book Launch
by Writers Publishing House

All rights reserved. No part of this book may be reproduced in any manner without written permission from the author except with brief quotations embodied in critical articles and reviews. The fact that an organization or website is referred to in this work as a citation and/or potential source of further information does not mean that the Author or the Publisher endorses the information, the organization, or website it may provide or recommendations it may make. Further, readers should be aware that websites listed in this work may have changed or disappeared between when this work was written and when it was read. Disclaimer: The cases and stories in this book have had details changed to preserve privacy.

Welcome Aboard

Remember YOU ARE LOVED
Melton Rackham

PT Boat 81 Still On WW II Nightmare Patrol

Dedicated To Those In WW II
Who Paid the Price
Of
Preserving America

Other Books by Myrl Thompson
myrlthompson.com

- Climbing Memory Mountain: From Down on the Farm, Into the World, and Back Again
- Skinny Little Frog
- Santa Does the Six Step
- Farm Song (by his daughter, Juli Dalton)
- The Dating Life of Mr. Clueless: Thoughts on Girls from the Old Swami
- Emma: The Last 100 Years

More Book by Myrl

Contents

Acknowledgments i

Foreword iv

Preface ix

Chapter 01 2
An Overview: Japan Attacks Pearl Harbor and Changes a Nation

Chapter 02 9
World War 11 Scars that Still Wake Me in the Night

Chapter 03 15
Boot Camp Was Over None Too Soon

Chapter 04 24
MacArthur Leaves the Philippines on a PT Boat Toward Australia....

Chapter 05 32
A Williwaw Welcome to Aleutian Bound PT Boats

Chapter 06 39
The First Day and Night of the Battle of Attu

Chapter 07 47
American Victory on Attu in Spite of Everything

Chapter 08 55
One Last Japanese Surprise in the Battle for Kiska

Chapter 09 60
One Last Look at the Aleutians Before We Leave

Chapter 10..68
Zeroes Interrupt our Moon-Light Cruise to the South Pacific

Chapter 11..73
Catching Up with the War in the South Pacific

Chapter 12..79
PT Boats Did Not Come With Luxury Accommodations

Chapter 13..84
Picking Up Military Intelligence and an Engine Full of Sand

Chapter 14..92
War is a Fiery Furnace that Forges the Character of Men

Chapter 15..100
If It's the Right Thing to Do, The Lord Knows How to Do It

Chapter 16..107
Time at the Bow of the Boat Before Night-Time Patrols

Chapter 17..114
PT Night Patrol in the Company of Unexpected Guests

Chapter 18..121
PT Boats Used as Troop Landing Craft

Chapter 19..131
KAMIKAZE - Port BOW

Chapter 20..139
The Evening of the Just-in-Case Notes to Our Mothers

Chapter 21..143
The Sky Full of Steel, Glass, and Whatever it Takes to Build a Ship

Chapter 22..**148**
Shrapnel Soaring like Steel Kites in the Sky

Chapter 23..**153**
An Empty Pail Floating in a Quiet South Pacific Sea

Chapter 24..**157**
From the End of PT-81 to the End of the WW II

Chapter 25..**164**
My Plan to Spend the Rest of My Life as a Hermit

Chapter 30..**172**
A New Kind of Night-time Dream

Epilogue..**177**
The Price of Liberty

Appendix **185**
Obituary **196**
Author Bio..**198**

Acknowledgments

To all my friends and to readers I have never met: Thank you for your patience with me. Time will tell whether I have been able to resolve my nightmare problem. Regardless of the personal result of my efforts, I am going to do everything I can to share the content of this book with as many people as possible, even if it is to reach just one person who may find help in what has been written.

To my best WWII friend: Thank you, Johnson, for all that you meant to me when we both lived and for the courage and caring you expressed by visiting me in my dream that night. Goodbye until we meet again, my friend. Until we meet again.

To my wife, Carol, I dedicate this book. It is my prayer that it will do its part in relieving you and me of the burden we have carried for so many years. I love you, sweetheart . . . for all time and eternity.

To my sons and daughters, grandsons and granddaughters: I testify to you of my love for your mother and grandmother, my love for each of you, and my love and faith in our Lord and Savior, Jesus Christ. Learn from the consequences of your choices. Beware of the adversary who will work to corrupt the blessing of free agency.

To my two friends, Morris Stuart and Myrl Thompson, who were on a mission one day to talk to me and get me to start talking back.

And finally, to my Savior, Jesus Christ, who has been with me through it all, even holding me in His arms when I could not see in my darkest hour.

A picture of me and my wife, Carol. When we began to date and discuss marriage, I told her that I was concerned about my PTSD symptoms and how they might negatively impact our family life. She told me she could handle it, and she surely has. I think it's because we like each other—a lot.

Foreword

It's hard to interview Milton Rackham. At 86, the Belding, Michigan resident's answers come slowly, deliberately, not because of his age, but because of the topic.

Rackham shares stories of the years he spent peering down the sights of a PT boat's big guns during World War II. Those stories, along with others of the ground action he experienced, offer a unique glimpse into a hell that those who have never known combat can scarcely imagine: moments when life and death collide, separated only by capricious fate, the trajectory of a bullet, a shard of shrapnel.

These are difficult stories to tell. It's only now, almost three-quarters of a century later, that Rackham can bring himself to talk about them at all.

For years after the war, he describes himself as a "flat-out basket case." All he wanted to do was remove himself from society, work, and try to forget. But putting the horrors of war behind him proved more difficult than he had imagined.

He eventually married a good woman willing to comfort him on the nights he woke screaming, hands locked viselike around the invisible grips of a 50-caliber turret, hammering round after round into the flight paths of approaching phantom Kamikazes.

Even now, after relating much of his experience to Big Rapids, MI author Myrl Thompson, there are things about which Rackham will not speak. "There are things that happen during wartime," Rackham tells me, "That are simply too grim to recall."

He leaves it at that, and no prodding will sway him.

Based on the stories had in Thompson's "PT-81 Still on WW II Nightmare Patrol", one can't help but think that this is for the best. Maybe there are some stories that are best left untold. Maybe the tales Thompson did convince Rackham to share should be enough for us.

Even though a therapist had advised him to share his stories with others, Milt was hesitant to talk about it when he and Thompson first started meeting. At first, the plan was to simply record his memories on a tape recorder for his family and his own healing. But before too long, it became clear this was a painful story that needed to be shared with the world.

The book evolved from there, moving from Rackham's experiences first in the Aleutian Islands, then in the Pacific Theater, and through his discharge and adjustment to civilian life. Along the way, Thompson uncovered the problems Rackham had obtaining GI benefits following the war. In what he calls typical military fashion, minor paperwork snafus, and an uncaring bureaucracy had conspired for 68 years to prevent Rackham from receiving the counseling and medical services he truly needed.

"Here I've got a Purple Heart hanging on my wall, and shrapnel in my body" Rackham says with a rueful smile, "but all my paperwork was ruined in some fire. So, I don't have any proof that I was actually injured."

Thompson dug in again and, with a flurry of letter writing to both the VA and his congressman, got Rackham's benefits reinstated at the age of 86.

The purpose of Thompson's book, however, is not to garner sympathy for disaffected vets. Instead, it is to tell an important story. He hopes it will help people understand in some small way what those men and women went through and what many are still going through.

"Talking with Rackham has been an experience and a half," Thompson relates. "To have this guy and all his memories at your disposal . . . we just want readers to understand what happened. We're just trying to create some awareness about what was going on."

"Our country really is worth this effort, I'll tell you that," Thompson said. "I started out as the poorest kid you can imagine; no indoor bathroom, a real social misfit. I wound up an executive engineer at General Motors. With this book, I'm looking for a way to pay back my country and its veterans for all they have done for me."

With the tales related in "PT Boat 81," Thompson has at least made a down payment on the debt he feels he owes. There is a richness to these stories that can come only from a first-hand account such as Rackham's. As for the chapters he cannot bring himself to relate, Rackham again asserts there are some things best left unwritten.

"It's like when I came home on leave that first time," Rackham says. "I got a 15-day pass and went to a dance. Some of the other kids came up to me and started asking things like, 'How many Japs did you kill?' I just turned around and walked right out of that building. I was done."

"Some things are …," Milt pauses to consider carefully. "… well … let's just say … the Lord and I have taken care of all that."

Michael Taylor,
The Daily News

Myrl Thompson (Left) sits down with Milt for the first time out in the Upholstery Shop.

Preface

WW II changed the lives of millions of men and women, including the life of one 17-year-old high school senior from Lorenzo, Idaho. My name is Milton Rackham, and I was that high school senior. Now, as an 86-year-old World War II veteran, I still carry with me the memories of fighting from the deck of U.S. Navy PT-Boat 81. Some of my battle scars have healed. Some still set off airport metal detectors when I travel, and others still wake me in the night.

So many in our nation have forgotten the personal price that was so willingly paid for them. And they are often unaware of the number of wartime veterans who silently continue to pay that price every single day.

Even now, when I awaken from my regular PTSD nightmares, the first thing I do is look around to catch sight of my wife. She is always standing beside our bed as I wake so that she can steer clear of my violent thrashing. She comes to me then, as she has so many times before. She reaches out and holds me as I cry, often uncontrollably, in her arms.

In 2007, I was advised that telling my story may help me to resolve my lifelong suffering. Shortly after that, my friend, Morris Stewart, came to my upholstery shop and introduced me to Myrl Thompson, a local author interested in writing my story. After we had been meeting for a while, Myrl submitted samples of my stories to the Big Rapids Pioneer, and they began running them in a weekly column in 2012.

I want to express how grateful I am for the opportunity to share my WW II experience, something that has been difficult for me. As Myrl and I have traveled and spoken to various groups, I have been surprised to find that some who have read my book have been healed of their own PTSD symptoms. And that has given me the will to keep sharing my story wherever I can.

Surely, there must be one person reading this out there who needs to know that they are not alone in trying to deal with wartime (or even non-wartime) memories that have disrupted their lives. I hope this project creates something useful for you while also helping ease the painful memories of war I've carried for so many years. May I be able to resolve the guilt I feel for having survived when so many others were taken time and time again, often within arm's length of where I stood. And may God bless both of us, you and I, whoever you are, that we will understand what the Lord would have us do from here.

Milton Rackham,
March, 2012

Milt Rackham

In Memory

PT-81 Crew Members on 4 Jan 1945

- JOHNSON, H.W. S1/c (TM) 802-10-71 USN - Killed.
- Lt (JG) R.H. DUNLAP, 268142, USNR - Minor shrapnel wound in RH Leg.
- Ensign J.W. Stitt, 206937, USNR - Concussion and bruises to the sacral region
- Ensign D.H. Hansen, 302181, USNR - Shrapnel - back, shoulder, fracture - LH shoulder
- JARVIS, W.L. QM 1/c, 300-78-37. USN - Shrapnel wound in back.
- ENGLISH, L.L. MOMM 1/c, 342-52-97, USN - Shrapnel wounds in back.
- PIRTLE, W. J., RM 1/c, 337-61-73, USN, Minor Shrapnel wound in right leg.
- BENNET, G.D., TM 2/c, 565-13-77, USN - Shock and minor shrapnel wound in the back.
- RACKHAM, M.(N), MoMM, 3/c 554-22-60, USNR - Minor shrapnel wounds in RH leg and LH arm.

- MCKUSTER, F. E., S 1/c (GM), 876-17-68, USN - Bruised right knee and leg.
- CUNNIGHAM, J.T. GM 3/c, 376-18-55, USN -Shrapnel wounds in both legs and feet
- TRAFTON, W.E., MoMM 2/c, 386-27-84, USN - Shock and minor Shrapnel wounds on the left side
- SMITH, M.L., MoMM 1/c,622-06-93, USN - Bruised Back
- KESTER., W. J., S1/c (GM), 806-35-87, USN - Minor shrapnel wound left arm and foot
- RYAN, J.J. S1/c(RoM), 887 47 58, USN - Minor bruises
- BISHOP, M.E., GM 3/c, 621-23-24, USNR - Minor Shrapnel Wounds - both legs

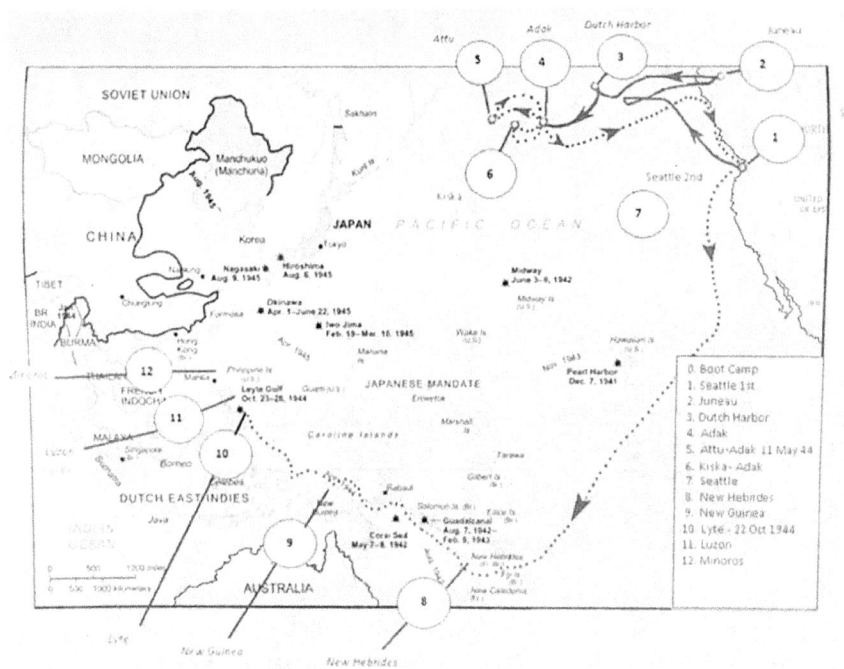

Milt Rackham WWII Journey

(1)
Aleutian Island Camp Site with nothing but rocks and frozen or wet Tundra as far as you could see. When the fog sets it, as far as you could see meant the length of your arm.

Chapter 01

An Overview: Japan Attacks Pearl Harbor and Changes a Nation

I'm an 86-year-old World War II Veteran who fought the war from the deck of U.S. Navy PT-boat 81. Some of my battle scars have healed, while others still set off airport metal detectors when I travel ... or wake me in the night.

It all started when waves of Japanese fighters, bombers, and torpedo planes flew over Pearl Harbor on Sunday, December 7, 1941. The United States was under attack in a surprise raid that destroyed a significant portion of the U.S. Pacific Fleet. The sequence of events that rapidly unfolded in the following hours, days, and weeks instantly changed the lives of millions of American men and women, including that of a 17-year-old high school senior in Lorenzo, Idaho. My name is Milton Rackham, and I was that high school senior.

Mere weeks after Pearl Harbor, I joined the U.S. Navy at the tender age of 17. My enlistment date was deferred to March 1942, which allowed me enough time to earn my high school diploma before leaving for boot camp. Months later, having survived that ordeal, I volunteered for PT boat duty, received additional training, and became part of the 17-man crew assigned to PT boat 81.

This 80-foot long, wood-hulled boat was what you could accurately imagine to be a glorified, very finely tuned, *very* heavily armed speedboat. And in the weeks that followed my training, it was to become my home away from home. Our first assignment took us far north to the Aleutian Islands, a 1,700-mile-long chain of islands that stretched 1,200 miles west through the Bering Sea from Alaska to the Russian coastline. Once our mission in the frozen north was complete, we would sail south to the South Pacific theater, where PT 81 and I would spend the rest of the war.

Until 1941, America had tried to ignore the war as it spread across Europe. But suddenly, we found ourselves deeply involved in two separate wars on opposite sides of the world. To make matters worse, the Japanese followed their attack on Pearl Harbor with a rapid, ongoing series of victories in the South Pacific, raising very real public concerns about a potential attack on the U.S. mainland itself.

Concerns about a Japanese invasion of our mainland proved to be well-founded. One of the war's best-kept secrets was that the U.S. had cracked the Japanese communications code early on. Unbeknownst to the public, military intelligence was busy intercepting daily reports indicating that Japanese advance scouting parties *had already landed* on U.S. soil and were quietly occupying the Aleutian Islands in preparation for an invasion of the mainland through Alaska. As you can imagine, U.S. military preparations to meet this threat were already well underway when I joined the war effort in the spring of '42.

I had made my decision to join the U.S. Navy after having seen the South Pacific war news reels at our local movie theater. Traveling in the opposite direction of the warm South Pacific islands was not exactly what I had in mind. But the threat was real, and we answered the call.

I was assigned to U.S. Navy PT boat 81, which was a part of RON-13, a 12-boat squadron that was scheduled to leave for the Aleutian Islands in August 1942. PT-81 and three other PT boats were pulled off the assembly line in New Orleans and scheduled for Navy-recommended design improvements that delayed delivery by three months. Unknown to me, PT-81 was to be lighter, faster, quieter, more durable, and more precisely lethal than anything previously seen in U.S. naval battle. As the war in the Pacific unfolded, these improvements would transform PT boats into a sort of sea version of the precision fighter planes you would see dogfighting with the enemy in the skies during the war.

We were scheduled to leave Seattle, Washington, on 10 May 1943 to join the rest of RON-13 already in the Aleutians. Our mission was to assist in the removal of the Japanese from that part of U.S. territory.

The Aleutian Islands campaign was to be a wet, cold, miserable experience for all concerned. Even the well-prepared Japanese, dressed in fur-lined uniforms and boots and living in tunnels and caves out of the weather, ended up suffering as U.S. forces eventually cut off their supply of food, ammunition, kerosene, and Saki.

Ground battles were often marked by the slow, agonizing advances of U.S. soldiers facing relentless hit-and-run sniper fire from entrenched Japanese positions scattered for miles beyond the landing beach. U.S. forces, often dressed in light uniforms and short, unlined boots, were completely unprepared for the freezing cold and hurricane-force winds that swept across the desolate Aleutian landscape day and night, even in August.

The final battle on the Aleutian Islands was a vicious encounter with Japanese suicidal Banzai attacks that historians rank second only in brutality to the Battle of Iwo Jima in the South Pacific.

Chapter 02

World War 11 Scars that Still Wake Me in the Night

The previous chapter provided an introductory glimpse of WW II as it unfolded against the Japanese in the North Pacific. Now, I'll provide you with just a snapshot of the war in the South Pacific. The material for this chapter will be based on my own nightmares, which have haunted me for the past 66 years.

Would you believe that, after having not had a war dream for over three months, I was awakened by one on the very night that I began tape recording for this book? Yes. And the dreams are intense. Would you come with me on a South Pacific WW II PT patrol so I can share the content of one of my dreams? I'll provide narration. Let your imagination provide surround-sound and Technicolor. That's the way my dreams are. Full sound. Full color.

We're patrolling along the shores of islands in the South Pacific, where the shipping lanes narrow and bring our Japanese supply ship targets within firing range. Our boats have a 6-foot draft, which allows us to stay close to shore, making it harder to spot us from sea or air. We keep our "backs to the wall" while we scan the ocean for targets and the sky for Japanese fighters.

There are 17 of us on PT-81, enough to man the boat, handle six cannons and machine guns, and enable torpedoes or dump depth charges. We are all trained to back each other up if the need arises.

We understand that we can be taken out either by enemy fire or by one of us being thrown overboard. Be careful; this boat accelerates to 42 knots in the time it takes you to breathe in and out once. That's 48 miles per hour for you land-locked folks.

Our three V-16 Packard gasoline aircraft engines are pumping 1,200 horsepower each. That's 3,600 horsepower hurtling us through the water on what amounts to a high-precision, heavily armed, highly lethal speedboat.

It banks hard on a dime. You'll get flipped overboard if you aren't careful, and believe me when Skipper is evading enemy fighters, you do NOT want to end up in the water as target practice for a Japanese pilot. I'll tell you about getting flipped overboard another time.

Listen! Hear that sound? Planes coming. You'll feel them before you hear them. And you'll hear them before you see them. There they are. Stand quietly. We need to find out if they see us this close to shore.

Ahhh . . . yup. They see us. Three this time. Turning our way. General quarters sounds. Get to battle stations and prepare your guns. We're going to be VERY busy in a few minutes. Once it starts, you're gonna be on your own.

Now that they've spotted us, our boat comes alive. Guns spin into position; our skipper guns the precision engines. We prepare for evasive maneuvers as our tracers mark the path of live ammunition we're pumping skyward toward the fighters.

The planes are lining up to strafe us. One plane breaks formation and begins its approach. Skipper darts the boat quickly out of their line of fire, and the plane roars by, strafing the now empty water with gunfire.

Now that he's gone by, he's a perfect target. Don't miss the chance to lock onto him. One of you has him in your sights. There's slight damage . . . wait . . . there's a barely visible, pencil-thin, black streak coming up and over his cockpit from the engine. Good Job! He'll head home rather than risk what might be an engine oil leak.

Second plane coming in. Skipper changes tactics, teasing the pilot this time with a long straight run. He dodges first one way, then the other, then away hard right. The fighter tries to follow our movements but flies wide at the speed he's traveling.

The now empty water where we just were is sprayed with Japanese gunfire. The plane roars past, its engine screaming like a mechanical bird of prey, angry at having missed us.

Another plane is coming at us now. This time from behind and higher up. Skipper throttles back, and the boat instantly slows and settles into the water. The fighter can't correct his speed that fast. He overshoots and banks into a turn-up ahead. This plane is so close that I can see the pilot... he turns, and we stare at one another.

In the split seconds that follow, first one, then two of our gunners lock the fighter in their gun sights. Ammunition and tracer fire puncture the fuselage from the cockpit to the tail with a staggered pattern of holes. The Japanese plane shudders, recovers, and then banks steeply upward. I can see the pilot's head and upper body lift slightly and turn. He's staring back as if he's trying to inspect the damage.

We continue to pellet the plane with ammunition as it continues its upward lift, unaware of the damage inflicted on its fuselage or upon its pilot, who is now slumped forward in his unshielded cockpit.

Suddenly, it's quiet. The planes are gone. We are alone! No, it's more than that! The entire scene is fading, and it's ME that's alone.

I'm sitting upright. My body is tense, my arms are rigid, with my tightly-clenched fists gripping an imaginary 50 cal. machine gun in front of me. I see something! I lock onto another incoming plane, and my entire body vibrates in time with the chatter of bullets spaced between tracer fire that arcs high into the sky.

Suddenly, I notice there are lights. This time, I realize I am sitting in bed. I turn to scramble out of bed and find my wife, Carol, beside me. She is stepping forward now that I have stopped thrashing. She reaches out to me as she has done so many times before.

I have just shared with you, as best I can, one of the nighttime war dreams that have been a part of my life for 66 years. I have lost track of the number of times I have relived these nightmares. For 61 of those years, Carol has shared these with me. I've spoken many times about my desire to resolve these thrashings, but my wife would probably like me to bring closure to my ongoing nighttime patrols even more than I do.

I warned her about me before our wedding, but she told me she could handle it, and she surely has. I remember that someone once asked her how she puts up with me. I loved her answer. She said, "I think it must be that we really like each other . . . a lot."

Who needs any more than to walk through life with someone like that, someone who is at your side when the horror of relived combat shatters the quiet of the night? Capturing and talking about this is a new experience for me. It will be interesting to see where this takes me from here.

Chapter 03

Boot Camp Was Over None Too Soon

I've now given you snapshots of my WW II PT boat experience in two different parts of the world: the cold, wet, windy North Pacific, where I started, and the South Pacific, where I served until the end of the war. I've also shared a little about the after-effects of the war-within-me. Now, it's time to go back and fill in a few details.

Before Pearl Harbor, the United States had mixed feelings about the war, ranging from isolationism to supporting allies with supplies. After Pearl Harbor, however, the country quickly united behind a common cause and declared war against the Axis in Europe and the Japanese in the Pacific.

Even before the war, I had already decided to join the Navy as soon as I turned 18. But, just weeks after Pearl Harbor, a friend on the local draft board let me know that my name was on the list to be drafted within days. If I really wanted to be in the Navy, I needed to get to the recruiting office ASAP.

After waiting for hours in line, I discovered that, at 17, I needed signed permission from my mother. I gathered the paperwork and headed home. After an emotional couple of hours, Mom disappeared to her bedroom. She came out five hours later with tear-stained eyes and her signature on the paperwork.

My recruiter signed me up for an enlistment that deferred boot camp until after I received my high school diploma. The high school accelerated my diploma, so I skipped graduation exercises. By March 1942, I was on a bus to boot camp in Farragut, Idaho.

I arrived to join a large group of young men fresh out of high school, many of whom had never been away from home for more than a weekend. The high-spirited, high-school chit-chat didn't last long. We were lined up and marched to our barracks the moment we arrived, and things went downhill from there during the next few weeks.

The first night, I couldn't sleep. It wasn't from fear of war or from the shock of being away from home but from the sounds of muffled sobbing and mournful cries that sounded from under pillows all up and down the barracks.

To my surprise, I was finding it a little easier to adjust to the shock of transitioning from civilian to military life. My experience of having been on my own the prior two summers with sheep and cattle herding jobs had given me a head start, which I was grateful for.

You won't be surprised to hear that boot camp included a rude awakening for anyone who was used to sleeping in. Revelry the next morning meant "Up-And-At-'Em-NOW." For those who remained unresponsive, our sergeant went down the rows of bunks, grabbing mattresses and flipping anyone still in bed out onto the floor.

I may have survived the first night a little better than most, but that was about all. My "head start" ran out of gas the second day after breakfast when we ended up in a room the size of a big gymnasium. I was so shy that I wasn't sure I was going to survive what happened next. We were lined up for medical inspections and shots, then ordered to strip right down to our undershorts. Let me tell you, I had no idea that ugly came in such a variety of shapes, sizes, heights, weights, and body hair until long lines of men started to strip down. I won't even mention the tattoos. They were beyond your imagination.

I had never been that close to being naked in front of anybody else in my entire life since I stopped wearing diapers. They wouldn't even let us leave our T-shirts on. Nobody else even seemed to mind, so I tried to pretend that I didn't either.

We stood in line for what seemed like hours. Some guys started to talk about what they inspected, where they put the shots, and how long the needle was. One great big, tall, muscle-bound dude a couple of spaces ahead of me kept bragging about how he wasn't afraid of anything.

All I could think of was that the last thing I wanted was to be inspected or poked by some guy. As I moved along in the line, however, I could finally see what was going on at the front and discovered that the inspectors were NOT guys. They were nurses - LADY nurses. And they were young. The closer I got to the front of the line, the faster it seemed to move, and before I knew it, it was over. The big muscle-bound braggart had passed out when the guy in front of him got his shot, and I had been grabbed, inspected, shot in the arm, and shuffled off to one side. I don't remember that my shot-giving nurse even said a word to me. I DO seem to remember that I was a little disappointed.

After a few weeks, the realization set in that we each had made more than just a commitment to leave the safety of home and family. We had made a commitment to dedicate our very lives to becoming members of the United States Navy. And we became honor-bound to accomplish whatever it was that they had in store for us. Boot camp inspections, strict rules, and obedience training moved us toward being a group that would soon have to depend on each other for our very survival.

The difficulty you faced during this attitude adjustment period depended on how fast you learned to listen. Here again, my experience of having been away from home for months at a time helped me at boot camp. Being at the bottom of the social totem pole with older, rough-and-tumble ranch hands turned out to have benefits I had not anticipated. If a sergeant breathed into my face, looked me in the eye, and said, "JUMP-MISTER!" I quickly learned not to even think of asking how high. You soon learned to say "Yes, SIR" and do what you were told. It was never a good idea to prolong the conversation.

I'll never forget an inspection called in our barracks as we were about to walk to the bus for our first leave since arriving. We lined up, all dressed and ready to board the bus. Sergeant came down the line, sometimes stopping and staring at someone, other times with questions and comments.

He got toward the end of the line and did a longer than usual stop-and-stare at one particular man. He finally stepped back and barked: "There is a man-aan in these ranks who does not meet the standard required to represent this group in public. Leave is hereby canceled for this otherwise very fine-looking group of United States Navy personnel. Diiiii-smissed!"

We could hardly believe he had just announced that leave was canceled . . . for everyone. He stalked off without another word, and the bus drove away without us.

There was dead silence. The poor fellow in question had come from very poor circumstances and had had problems with hygiene from day one. He had been taken aside and talked to more than once. I knew he had been trying, but I also knew he still had a ways to go.

Everyone was upset. Most just said a few choice words and walked away. I felt sorry for him, so you can imagine I was not prepared for what happened next. One group of four gathered, spoke quietly for a minute or two, and then walked over to the man. They picked him up and carried him kicking and screaming to the shower, clothes and all. I sat on my bunk as chaos reigned in the shower room. The poor man fought tooth and nail. There was yelling, screaming, and profanity. After fifteen minutes, he suddenly appeared in the hallway, naked, glowing red all over, and cleaner than he had probably ever been. His wad of wet clothes followed seconds later, hit the wall, and slid down to the floor in a puddle. Last of all, a couple of stiff-bristled toilet brushes also came flying out of the shower, hit the wall, and went rattling down the hallway.

We survived boot camp and arrived at graduation in white, full dress uniform, our rifles and everything else polished and gleaming in the sun. The ceremony included 4,000 graduates from different sites marching in groups of 200. As each group passed the review stand, they broke into well-practiced precision marching patterns to the barking commands of their sergeant.

As our PT group arrived in front of the stand, we initiated our marching performance. The loudspeaker came to life and proudly made an announcement. It created a warm feeling of loyalty to my country and a readiness to fight anyone who would dare seek to destroy her. I don't remember the exact words, but let me paraphrase the loudspeaker announcement for what happened next.

"Ladies and gentlemen, let me tell you that from my view up here high on the review stand, these 4,000 men are a magnificent sight. I have never seen a finer force of navy graduates more prepared and eager to defend their country. Join me in an ovation of appreciation as I say to them, well done, young sailors . . . and may God be with you in the days ahead until our job is done."

The crowd roared with appreciation. No one, except a few within our group of 200 (and probably our sergeant), noticed that one of us made a mistake during a "Ri-i- Iight-FACE" command in our performance. He was late in his maneuver, and there was a loud "Crack" as a right-spinning rifle butt-smacked him in the head. He didn't miss a step and survived with no more than one very black eye and a lump on his forehead.

The graduation ceremony will be forever bright in my memory. But boot camp itself was over none too soon. I found myself assigned to PT-81 as part of RON-13, a squadron of twelve PT boats. We were scheduled to head north rather than south to join the war.

Chapter 04

MacArthur Leaves the Philippines on a PT Boat Toward Australia

At the time we left boot camp, Japanese forces were not only occupying U.S. territories off the coast of mainland Alaska. They were also advancing unchecked across the Philippines in hopes of capturing General MacArthur.

MacArthur was slow to leave and missed U.S. planes and Navy ships that had been waiting for him on standby. When he ended up stranded in the face of an advancing enemy, PT boats were called in to remove him, his family, and his staff in a last-minute rescue.

Not many people know that, while the general made his famous "I shall return" speech, PT boat captains were scrambling behind the scenes to plot a course toward Australia to get him out of there. Charting the nighttime island-hopping course for their highly visible passenger was complicated. This was to be their maiden voyage toward Australia across an ocean dotted with islands that were unnamed on their maps. And there was always the possibility that MacArthur might be picked up anywhere along the way and taken by air once they had cleared him of the war zone, which was now overrun with Japanese.

The PT boats and their 3600 HP engines carried 3,000 gallons of fuel and had a range of only 500 miles between fill-ups. The skippers had never charted a course for Australia before, so strategically planning fuel supplies along the way became an important part of the trip.

Several PT crewmen who had traveled with the MacArthur group ended up assigned to our squadron, so we got a first-hand, blow-by-blow description of the MacArthur evacuation. We also got a good description of the Army-Navy rivalry that flared between MacArthur aides and PT boat skippers in charge of the operation.

Apparently, the aides became alarmed when they discovered the lack of detailed information available for the mission. They received little solace from the skippers, who were busy trying to chart a course for their first-ever trip to Australia with MacArthur's aides hovering and fussing over their shoulders.

Below is an exchange between Army aides and the busy Navy PT boat captains, as best as can be remembered from stories 66 years after the fact. Even though I was not a part of the MacArthur mission, I want to include the story we were told because it serves as a good example of the "jack of all trades" lifestyle that all PT boat captains and crew members lived on a daily basis.

> Aide: (pointing to a dot on a map) "What's the name of that island?"
>
> Skipper: (shrugging) "I don't know."
>
> Aide: "Is it inhabited?"
>
> Skipper: "I don't know."
>
> A: (sputtering) "Are <u>any</u> of these islands inhabited?"
>
> S: "I don't think so."
>
> A: "So, where will you get gas for the trip?"
>
> S: "Every 500 miles."
>
> A: "Yes, yes . . . But how does it get there?"
>
> S: "It's dropped off by another PT boat or a PT supply ship."

A: "It just sits there?? By itself? What if the Japanese find it.?"

Apparently, at this point, one of the skippers couldn't stand it any longer and shut down the questioning with an abrupt presentation:

"Okay, okay, you guys." (counting on his fingers) "Listen up. We travel at night. We find plotted islands at night, in pitch dark. We do it all the time. That's why we are here. We are very busy plotting a course and selecting islands we think we can reach between fill-ups. We order fuel ahead of time for those stops. We stop at islands and camouflage the boat before sunrise. Nobody goes anywhere in the daytime. We stay on the camouflaged boat and silent until the sun goes down. There are zero restaurants, no bars, and NO places of entertainment anywhere along the trip. PT boats do NOT have bathrooms. The Pacific Ocean is our bathroom."

"No," he continued his tirade, "we are not going to take port-a-potties for the trip. Yes, falling off the boat while using the ocean as a bathroom at 50 mph is possible. If you fall overboard, it is unlikely that we'll be able to find you in the dark. If we can't find you right away, we'll have to leave you in the water so we can keep to our nighttime travel schedule."

"If you are following our instructions, you will all be wearing life preservers. We'll send a sub to come and look for you later. Just don't do anything that attracts sharks while you're waiting."

There was an uncomfortable silence, followed by a question from one brave MacArthur aide.

A: "Have you PT guys ever made this trip to Australia before?

S: "No."

A: "Then how in hell are you going to get us to Australia if you don't know where you're going and how to get there?"

S: "Who says we don't know where we are going? Didn't you say you wanted to go to Australia? Okay, so we are going to Australia. We will get there. That's what we do. But we aren't going anywhere if you don't let us get this job done and get the fuel deliveries scheduled."

"By the way, what is it that YOU guys do in this war? Whatever it is, it is NOT getting done with you standing here, so why don't you get your buns out of here and go do your job? We need to get out of here before the Japanese figure out that we have you and decide to send someone over to get your boss."

"We are more than happy to transport you any place, any time of the day or night, but if you are unhappy with the service being provided, may I suggest that next time you do a better job getting your guy on board one of the half dozen planes and ships with BATHROOMS that you have waiting on standby for him? After all, it was YOUR job to get him out of here . . . wasn't it?"

Ultimately, MacArthur made his night-time PT boat trip with only a few incidents. At one point, his boat got separated from the group and fell behind in the dark of the moonless night. As it tried to catch up, the crew neglected to acknowledge coded signals, and the lead boat thought an enemy patrol boat might be approaching.

Not wanting to fire at the incoming vessel in case it was McArthur, the crew ended up dumping hundreds of gallons of fuel in an effort to lighten their load and gain speed to evade the approaching boat. This, of course, meant that there wasn't enough fuel to get all the PT boats to the next refueling island, so one of them had to be sunk to avoid giving the Japanese daylight air patrols any clue as to where MacArthur might be.

The bottom line was that, despite what his aides might have thought, MacArthur arrived in Australia with a high regard for PT boats and their capabilities in both battlefront and subversive operations. As soon as he reached Australia, he placed an order for the urgent delivery of 200 more to be brought to the South Pacific, with specific instructions to include a list of upgrades and improvements recommended by the officers and men on the front lines of the war at sea.

The Navy could not possibly deliver such a large-scale order in the short term. However, it immediately removed four PT boats from the assembly line and made the upgrades and design changes MacArthur requested. It also ramped up its recruiting efforts for PT crewmen, and it was this major push that caught my attention as I left boot camp. I ended up volunteering for PT boat service, was transferred to Rhode Island for additional training, and then assigned as the engine specialist to PT-81. Our new naval "home away from home" was one of those four much-improved, more heavily armed, more reliable, higher-performing vessels that MacArthur had requested in the spring of '42.

Chapter 05

A Williwaw Welcome to Aleutian Bound PT Boats

Soon after my additional training, I was set to disembark from Seattle, Washington, with orders to report to a base in the Aleutian Islands alongside my crewmates. However, at the last minute, I ended up in a Seattle hospital with an ear infection that needed emergency attention, and my PT-81 crewmates left without me. Two days later, I boarded a two-engine Navy plane departing Seattle and heading north to rendezvous with PT-81 and the three other upgraded PT boats traveling with it.

Ordinarily, a two-day hospital stay and a few extra hours of flight time wouldn't be worth mentioning. Here, however, it sets the stage not only for our North Pacific war with the Japanese but also for another ongoing battle against our second enemy, the relentless fury of the North Pacific weather.

Before I even arrived, it was obvious to me that this second enemy was determined to sweep both Japanese and U.S. forces off the Aleutians entirely and into the depths of the North Pacific Ocean. After five hours in the air, flying in increasingly bad weather, we found that we could not land at our intended destination. This meant retracing our flight path back toward Seattle and looking for someplace else to land. After several more tense hours in the air, we made an emergency landing in Juneau, Alaska, a small town where we spent four days waiting for the storm to pass.

Once we were safely on the ground, we learned that we had just experienced a relatively common typhoon-like storm, locally referred to as a *Williwaw*. When the storm finally let up enough for us to inspect our plane, we found that ours was the only one left outside. All other planes were either in hangars or securely covered with large tents, tarps, and anything else that could protect them from the driving snow.

It didn't take long to discover what this new enemy, called the *Williwaw,* was capable of. Its swirling, 125 MPH hurricane-force winds had driven snow, sleet, ice, and dirt deep into every single crevice of our plane. It was filled from stem to stern, top to bottom, and side to side with hard-packed snow and debris. For the next several days, we used chisels and screwdrivers to chip away hard-packed snow from every crack, crevice, wire, and space around the engines in the two separate engine compartments.

We dug snow from around all controls, landing gear, door latches, and keyholes. We shoveled, chiseled, brushed, and swept snow from everywhere inside the cockpit and throughout the passenger compartment, which was packed from floor to ceiling.

Meanwhile, the rest of our crewmembers had been facing the effects of the same storm with their PT boats strapped to the deck of a massive cargo ship, riding 30-foot waves on the open sea. With no cargo hold below deck on the cargo ship, their only protection from the weather had been the small PT chart houses above deck, or the PT holds, which offered nothing more than a galley and a hard plank floor.

Wooden-hulled and newly improved, the PT boats proved to be remarkably durable in the storms. Hunkering down in them on 30-foot seas, however, turned out to be a dangerous undertaking for my fellow crewmembers.

Going below deck became impossible. In one incident, a crewman took the first step from the PT deck into its hold and found that the cargo ship carrying them had suddenly dropped 30 feet below where he had been standing. He instantly fell into the hold of his PT boat, only to find that the cargo ship was now rising on the next wave, traveling at high speed. The rising boat met him halfway while he was still in midair. He hit the bottom of the hold with a force that broke his leg, and the 30-foot waves tossed him around inside the hold like a ping-pong ball. A second crewman began to make his way into the hold to rescue the first, and he also ended up injured, this time with a broken arm.

As the number of injuries continued to mount, the Navy eventually solved the problem by issuing an order (as if paperwork would solve everything). From then on, all hands received orders to stay top-side during a *Williwaw* when waves were 30 feet or greater.

The four PT boats survived the North Pacific storms with their crews a little worse for wear and arrived at Dutch Harbor (a point on the Aleutian chain located about 1000 miles west of the Alaska mainland) in May 1942. My flight, which had been stranded in Juneau, took advantage of a break in the weather and delivered me to Dutch Harbor so I could rejoin my crewmates on PT-81.

We spent four days in Dutch Harbor, a small Alaskan fishing outpost that had become a fortified army site where the

U.S. continued to receive and decode vital Japanese military information. The site was heavily armed with anti-aircraft weapons and manned with a minimal staff to keep it fully operational.

Most people don't realize that Pearl Harbor was not the only site on U.S. soil that was subjected to aerial attack during World War II. Just one month after we passed through there, Dutch Harbor was bombed twice by the Japanese. The bombings were part of a larger Japanese plan to land troops at three locations along the string of Aleutian Islands to the west.

On June 3, 1942, the first Japanese bombers left their carriers on a flight toward Dutch Harbor. The weather turned bad, and a majority of the planes either turned back or went down in the storm. Those who did arrive were surprised to find plenty of U.S. anti-aircraft fire from the ground and U.S. fighter planes in the air. They quickly emptied their bomb racks and left with little damage being inflicted on the U.S. harbor.

The next morning, on June 4, a second Japanese wave arrived and was again faced with anti-aircraft fire and fighter planes waiting to meet them in the air.

The Japanese held their course that second time as part of assessing U.S. military strength in the area and did much more damage on the ground. Through these two incidents, the Japanese realized that they lost the element of surprise and had underestimated the existence of air bases and the presence of U.S. troops in the region.

What the Japanese didn't realize was that their original scouting information had actually been correct. However, the U.S. had rushed the construction of U.S. Air bases because of their ability to decode Japanese messages and catch up to their plans.

It was under these circumstances that we made our own final approach to our theater of engagement: the Battle of Attu.

Dutch Harbor in the Aleutian Island after Japanese Bomers were surprised to find American Fighter Planes arriving to meet them. They quickly dropped their bombs to lighten their loads and left.

Chapter 06

The First Day and Night of the Battle of Attu

I first saw action in the Battle of Attu. The U.S. had been successful in repelling an aerial attack on Dutch Harbor. Still, the plan to quickly sweep occupying ground troops from Attu met with obstacles beyond anything U.S. military planners had anticipated.

The combination of severe weather, difficult terrain, and well-prepared Japanese troops was eventually overcome only by the perseverance of American troops and incidents of exceptional courage and heroism by individual soldiers. The price of victory in the North Pacific was high.

The battle for Attu, which had been postponed from August 1942 until 10 May 1943, was delayed again an additional six days by the weather. We made a landing on 16 May 1943 and were intent on a quick victory.

The basic plan was to engage and rapidly overwhelm the enemy with a larger force. U.S. forces were lightly dressed and lightly equipped to facilitate this rapid advance inland without the added weight of heavier clothing, boots, and gear.

Supply trucks, mobile artillery, and support vehicles were ready to land on command in support of what was expected to be a swiftly moving ground force of U.S. personnel.

The attack was initiated with a bombardment from the "Mighty Mo" (the battleship Missouri) and other support ships that sat offshore. The bombardment lasted for hours. U.S. planes bombed and strafed the beachhead while U.S. bombers flew inland and dropped a tremendous load on the Japanese encampments.

Although the Japanese inland encampments themselves were completely leveled, the caves and tunnels where the Japanese actually lived beyond the reach of the bitter *Williwaw* remained untouched. As a result, almost the entire Japanese force that had originally landed on Attu was still intact.

The battle plan next engaged our small, light PT boats up and down the coastline. Early in the war, PT boats were considered "expendable." Skipper ordered us to fire inland, not to do damage, but rather to draw out return enemy fire that would create fire flashes as targets for the heavier guns that were sitting offshore. Because of our swiftness and maneuverability, we remained untouched in a dozen passes back and forth in front of enemy squads hidden along the shore.

Not all of our PT boats were as fortunate as PT-81 was. One drew heavy Japanese cannon fire as it attempted to outrun the barrage. U.S. ships offshore promptly laid shells into the enemy fire flashes, but it was too late to save them. PT-219 was hit and destroyed as its 3000-gallon gas tanks split open and exploded.

Meanwhile, PT-81 had already played a critical role in the landing, but the invasion itself was just beginning. Landing craft followed, and U.S. troops (many of them just 18 years old like myself) hit the beach and began to move inland under relatively light enemy fire. Supply trucks, personnel carriers, and mobile artillery landed on the beach and prepared to follow.

The vehicles struggled through the loose beach sand and finally reached the Aleutian muskeg (bog or swamp), hoping for better traction. Instead, they came to a stop less than 100 yards from the beach, each buried up to its axles in wet, muck-like muskeg 12 to 24 inches deep.

The beach became a parking lot. Meanwhile, lightly dressed, lightly supplied U.S. troops moved inland without them, their only resistance being the same landscape that had stalled the vehicles. The muskeg tangled and tripped running feet and slowed them down until their paths wore all the way down to the frozen permafrost below. The path turned into a slippery layer of mud over frozen soil and then into an oppressive mire as hundreds of soldiers made their way inland.

The relatively light resistance at the beach seemed too good to be true, and it was. U.S. observers watched the lack of Japanese resistance, looking for confirmation that the initial bombardment had done its job. But the ridges and hilltops along the valleys that led inland were dotted with trenches, each occupied by a Japanese sniper camouflaged to avoid detection from the air. They had orders to hold their fire until U.S. Soldiers had fully entered the valleys and distanced themselves from their supplies, which were still mired back at the landing beach.

When the Japanese snipers did start firing, our young Soldiers were sitting ducks. They scattered in every direction, looking for cover on the barren landscape. Rocks were everywhere, but none were big enough to hide behind. U.S. Soldiers were pinned to the frozen ground that continued to melt and refreeze beneath them.

The weather and its ally, the Aleutian landscape, had joined in the battle and began taking its toll on U.S. forces on the very first night of the invasion. The lightly dressed, lightly supplied U.S. troops had no choice but to prepare for nightfall. The sun set at 10 PM, giving the men only four short hours of cover in the frigid Aleutian summer night. The temperature plummeted, and the mire began to freeze. As long as there was even a hint of daylight, Japanese snipers continued to fire from their trenches perched high above the tragedy unfolding in the valley below.

As the sun rose at 2 AM the next day, courageous individual U.S. Soldiers who had flanked the sniper positions in the dark of night looked down into the trenches only to find them empty. The Japanese had anticipated discovery in the night and had moved on just far enough ahead to continue firing.

Sniper trenches on the island of Attu

The ridges and hill tops on the Aleutian Island of Attu were dotted with Japanese sniper trenches.

U.S. Soldiers making their way inland on Attu ... with dug in snipers waiting for them up ahead.

Chapter 07

American Victory on Attu in Spite of Everything

Sunrise came at 2 AM. It found U.S. forces in a very difficult situation as they prepared to face the second day of the invasion. Once the soldiers had left the beach and moved inland, they were beyond the protective firepower of our PT boats. For the next 17 days, we turned our attention instead to whatever needed to be done to assist with the landing. We stood by to receive and transport the wounded or anyone else who would soon begin to return from the battlefront.

By the end of the second day on Attu, our foot soldiers were facing a tough situation. When the wounded began to arrive, they provided us with blow-by- blow descriptions of the battle. The stories they told us, along with the carnage we saw firsthand, still haunts my heart and mind.

The muskeg was cold and wet year-round, and our soldiers were soon soaked to the skin through their lightweight uniforms and boots. Frostbite and disease began to rapidly take their toll.

U.S. Soldiers haul supplies inland from supply trucks swamped in the muskeg on the landing beach. We often assisted with foot transport when bad weather kept us ashore.

The battle lasted eighteen miserable days. As time went on, U.S. shortages of ammunition, water, and food began to occur at the battlefront. All the supplies needed to sustain our troops were still sitting in trucks stuck along the edges of the landing beach and had to be carried inland on foot from the trucks to the front lines.

Soldiers and any other available personnel were on hand to assist. Some supplies, such as a tripod-mounted 50 caliber machine gun, required at least two, preferably three, men to carry through the muskeg and across the Aleutian hills and valleys.

We PT crewmembers often assisted with supplies when bad weather kept us ashore. And as difficult as the landscape was, that was just the beginning. Japanese snipers constantly targeted those of us carrying supplies as soon as we came within range.

American Soldiers had been issued only light clothing and were not dressed for the cold, wet Aleutian weather. As soon as we discovered that the Japanese were much better prepared for the cold, it wasn't long before our men began to appear wearing long, fur-lined coats, sturdy, fur-lined high-top boots, and scarves and gloves of Japanese issue. They risked their lives in headlong, surprise charges up a ridge and into a sniper's trench, sometimes just to take his clothing, and his life if necessary.

Two U.S. Soldiers demonstrate uniform styles found in the Aleutians. Soldier left wears a U.S Army light jacket and low-cut boots. Soldier right wears a knee-length, fur-lined coat and sturdy high-top boots of Japanese issue, probably taken from its owner by force. Isn't that a hint of fur lining sticking out between the left boot and the tucked-in trousers?

One World War II story tells of a starving Japanese sniper who noticed that Japanese uniforms were becoming increasingly common in U.S. military camps. Freezing and starving himself, he crept into the camp in the dark of night and joined an American chow line. His Japanese gear fit right in and he moved right along as the line advanced toward the mess tent. But he blew his cover when he tried to join a discussion about the winning records of American baseball teams and was caught associating the wrong players with the wrong teams.

The victory we eventually won in the Battle of Attu was the result of unrelenting pressure. Our larger force slowly pushed Japan's smaller forces from one trench, hole, cave, or tunnel to another while operating from unprotected positions ourselves. Equally important were the numerous incidents of open, heroic charges by individual U.S. Soldiers into the face of sniper fire and Japanese grenades. They would rise up out of the cold mud after being pinned down for sometimes hours at a time. The whole time, PT-81 assisted with the transport of supplies and mangled men.

The part of WWII that was fought in the Aleutians has been called by some *The War of Frustration*. Nearly 3,000

American and Japanese Soldiers died there. Military planners made poor assumptions when basic facts about landscape, weather, and battle conditions were available for the asking. Because of this, it was an unnecessary disaster measured in lives lost. American fathers and sons, as well as those at home, paid a high price for a victory in a part of the world few to this day even know exists.

Realize, too, that, at the time of the invasion, we had already cut the Japanese supply lines to the area. In many ways, a victory was already in the cards as the Japanese were becoming increasingly starved of food, ammunition, kerosene, and Saki. Because of this, many war historians still argue today that victory at Attu could have been more comfortably obtained simply by waiting it out.

But, the way it played out, Japanese frustration began to mount as they recognized the futility of ongoing battles. Fortifying themselves with Saki, they prepared for a final Banzai attack, which came on the night of May 28, 1943. U.S. scouts were appalled to witness hundreds of Japanese soldiers stripped to the waist and dancing around huge bonfires in a screaming, Saki-induced frenzy. They raced back to their leadership, running through front lines, barracks, and triage areas yelling warnings about what was coming.

But they could not get there in time. On May 29, just minutes after they arrived in American-held territory, a screaming rush of what was left of the now-suicidal Japanese army became the tip of a spear that initiated a hand-to-hand fight to the death. They swept through U.S. battle lines, medical tents, and construction areas where Soldiers, medical personnel, engineers, and anyone who could find a rifle, bayonet, or kitchen knife fought for their lives.

The slaughtered bodies of both U.S. and Japanese Soldiers were strewn everywhere. Historians now rank the Battle of Attu second only in brutality to the Banzai attacks experienced in Iwo Jima. So ended what turned out to be a U.S. victory in the Battle of Attu.

Chapter 08

One Last Japanese Surprise in the Battle for Kiska

U.S. military planners had been surprised by what had happened to the forces in the Battle of Attu. The level of Japanese military planning and preparedness, their knowledge and use of the Aleutian weather and landscape to their advantage, and the final suicide attack were only a few of the surprises that had contributed to the high price paid for the American victory on Attu.

The next operation was to be the invasion of the island of Kiska, the last Japanese stronghold in the Aleutian Island chain. U.S. military planners did not want a repeat performance of the Attu experience, so they redoubled their efforts using what they had learned. They laid out a plan for Kiska, confident there would be no more surprises.

The American attack on Kiska would not be a repeat of the Battle for Attu but it would end up revealing one last Japanese surprise.

U.S. preparation for the Battle of Kiska

"Expendable" PT-81 and our counterparts were once again to serve as decoys. They fitted us with mocked-up plywood silhouettes to make it appear like a two-pronged invasion, with the intent of spreading Japanese defenders over two separate beaches. U.S. forces launched an aerial attack first and, as the bombardment subsided, received a second indication of not only a lack of Japanese resistance but also a lack of any sign of Japanese forces in aerial photos from the returning bombers. Requests for confirmation were issued, and the reply indicated no sign of enemy forces.

U.S. military leaders paused and decided that if the Japanese were secreted in the caves and tunnels known to exist, they would still have to be hunted down and removed. If they really were gone, then the operation would be a valuable "training lesson" that would prepare U.S. Soldiers for other upcoming island operations in both the South Pacific and Italian theaters of war.

And so, the invasion was on.

34,000 U.S. Soldiers landed with no enemy resistance. They moved inland expecting Japanese snipers that never materialized. History records that U.S. and Canadian troops ultimately arrived at Japanese camps and found them defended by four starving dogs and one dead soldier who had been left behind.

Thousands of Japanese troops evacuated using transports between 28 July and early August, during the time the U.S. was involved in battle preparations. Our troops searched miles of tunnels, confirmed that the Japanese were gone, and pronounced the Island of Kiska to be back in the hands of the U.S. on 15 August 1943.

The price of "victory" in the Kiska operation was 313 U.S. Soldiers killed in action by friendly fire. Based on their recent experience on the island of Attu, two separate U.S. and Canadian units were expecting to encounter the Japanese at any moment on their inland march. When they sighted each other, they mistakenly thought they had finally discovered the enemy and opened fire.

Incredibly, neither unit had been told that bombing photos had indicated that the Japanese had already left the island prior to the invasion.

For the total Aleutian operation, the U.S. deployed 144,000 U.S. Soldiers against 8,500 Japanese at a U.S. price for victory of 1,481 killed, 3,416 wounded, and 640 missing. The Japanese price for their attempt to keep the Aleutians was 4,350 killed, 28 captured, and an unknown number wounded and missing.

WWII in the Aleutians was over, but for us, the war was just beginning. In September 1943, RON-13 left for Seattle as the first step in our travel to the South Pacific. The South Pacific was still dominated by the Japanese, who were winning battle after battle, and the need for PT boats, especially the redesigned versions like PT-81, was urgent.

Chapter 09

One Last Look at the Aleutians Before We Leave

I've given you the history. Now it's time for one final look at Milton Rackham's personal Aleutian experience.

On the off chance that you, too, may want to someday "go camping" in the Aleutian Islands, here is a little travel advice that my writer, Myrl Thompson, found on the internet.

This is written by someone who is familiar with the island of Adak, where our Aleutian home base was located:

"The Williwaw focuses its way through mountain valleys and accelerates by temperature changes. It starts at close to 60 knots and tops out at speeds that rip anemometers off towers, so nobody knows what its top speeds can be. It rips roofs off buildings. It will rip the doors off your car. I have seen the wind send steel garbage dumpsters tumbling down the road. It has pushed my car out of the parking lot, across the street, and into a ditch at Birchwood barracks. It has sent me flying through the air (fun, but dangerous, like the day I decided to "hang glide" using only my parka. Worked like a charm.).

RAIN FALLS SIDEWAYS - NEVER DOWN. Many days I arrived at work soaking wet on one side of my body and dry on the other. You get disoriented because the whole world is moving sideways -- or perhaps you are the one moving sideways -- which is it?

Driving is prohibited in a *Williwaw* except for emergency vehicles. That loud clunk you just heard might be a huge snow blower chopping up the car that you abandoned on the road because you could not see where you were going. I spent thirty minutes once driving just one block from the hangar to Birchwood barracks. I did it entirely by feeling for the drifts on the side of the road left by the snowplow. Those same drifts could not be seen despite being right outside the car windows.

Never go alone. Watch out for left-over booby traps from World War II. Want fun? Pitch a tent in 40+ knot winds. Want more fun? Take it down and try to roll it up in the same wind!"[1]

---

[1] orneveien.org/adak/description.htm

As far as we were concerned, in late 1943, the enemy had pulled out, and our job was done in this wretched part of the world. We returned to Adak for some recovery time in preparation for leaving for Seattle. Arriving in Adak, we tied the boats securely to the dock, and began carrying belongings toward our barracks just as a renewed onslaught of *Williwaw* winds came crashing down the steep mountain slopes. Snow and ice blowing at hurricane speeds reduced visibility to the length of my arm by the time we reached the barracks.

Our recovery time in Adak was anything but deluxe. We entered the barracks, which turned out to be a Quonset hut, a prefabricated steel building notorious the world over for being cold in the winter and hot in the summer. Two kerosene heaters, one at each end, burned on their highest settings 24 hours a day, but the temperature inside our barracks ranged from cold at the level of the upper bunks to sub-freezing at the lower ones. Men in the top bunks were comfortable in navy-issue sleeping bags and blankets. By contrast, those in the lower bunks had trouble keeping warm even with double and triple layers of navy-issue blankets and sleeping bags, plus whatever else they could find to pile on top. These buildings were obviously intended for a campaign that had been expected to be completed in a few weeks at most, not 14 months.

As bad as our barracks were, our situation was nothing when compared to what our U.S. Army troops had faced on the battlefield. The stories of the returning wounded were still fresh in our minds; stories of Soldiers forced to sleep in the open at night in subzero temperatures, dressed in light summer uniforms and light boots, in an Aleutian landscape where there was little if any naturally available fuel for a campfire.

Stored away in my memory forever is the story of four U.S. front-line soldiers found huddled dead around a campfire. Inside the fire ring were the remnants of their half-burned wooden rifle butts, their only source of fuel, in an unsuccessful attempt to survive the rage and fury of the *Williwaw*.

Visibility in Adak was so poor that we tied ropes from our barracks to the latrines and between the barracks and the mess hall. We clung to them wherever we went just to keep from losing our way. One of our earliest fatalities was a man who refused to use the ropes. He disappeared one night on the way from the barracks to the mess hall, and a scouting team found him two days later during a break in the winds. After having survived a war zone, they found him at our home base not far from our barracks, frozen to death.

On one occasion in the mess hall, I set my plate of food on the table, and as I began to sit down, I watched it suddenly slide across the table, become airborne, and crash against a wall 20 feet away. The entire opposite end of the mess building (another Quonset hut) was blowing inward from the hurricane-like winds. The freezing arm of a *Williwaw* reached in through the opposite end of the mess building (which was now completely caved-in) and began filling the building with blinding snow and ice.

Our first enemy, the Japanese, had left in defeat. Our second enemy, with its vicious, icy arm, seemed to be reminding us that we were not welcome there either.

It was past time to be leaving. We only spent a few days at Adak in the barracks on shore, but it was more than enough. We were eager to leave the North Pacific behind us and head south. Visibility in the open North Pacific Ocean was no better than on shore, sometimes allowing you to see at a distance no greater than the length of your arm.

As we approached the Alaska coastline at the base of the Aleutian Chain, Skipper noticed that we were approaching the entrance to the Inland Water Way. He radioed RON-13 that PT-81 and two other PT boats were leaving the squadron for a detour past the glaciers that lined the waterway. We broke away from the rest of the squadron that remained at sea.

It wasn't clear how he managed the special permission required to make such a pleasure trip, but none of that was our concern. The scenery was breathtaking. I had never seen anything like it before in my 18-year-old life. Miles of green glacial ice rose hundreds of feet high along a wide waterway. Icebergs were floating everywhere, having "calved" from the glaciers that moved just inches per year on their journey to the sea.

The only things missing on our pleasure cruise were heated staterooms, private bathrooms with tubs and showers, beds with mattresses and pillows and warm quilts, lavishly spread tables of fine food, dance floors, and game rooms. Other than that, it was a dream tour after what we had been through in the Aleutians.

Two days later, we were in Calder Bay when a *Williwaw* swept down and tore the chart house off PT-81. The chart house was the enclosure on the deck of a PT boat that housed the controls, the skipper, and the maps and charts required for navigation. We were delayed for two weeks while we waited for a new one to be flown in on a Lockheed P-38 that landed on pontoons.

Now that our tour was over and we had a new chart house, we left the Aleutians forever and headed for Seattle. The next theater of engagement was to be the South Pacific. It was anticipated to be warmer both in terms of the weather as well as the heat U.S. forces were taking from the Japanese, who continued to hold the upper hand in that part of the world.

Chapter 10

Zeroes Interrupt our Moon-Light Cruise to the South Pacific

Having completed our tourist-class cruise of the Inland Waterway between Alaska and the United States coastline, we now joined the rest of our squadron in Seattle, Washington. We received our orders to ship out to the South Pacific.

PT-81 was loaded onto the deck of a merchant marine freighter and strapped into place for the seven-day trip to our next theater of operations. Each of these four freighters carried four PT boats each. Our four specially-modified boats had been strategically placed so they could be used for protection in the event it was needed. The first several days after leaving Seattle were a warm continuation of our colder tour down the Inland Waterway. We were still traveling tourist class, this time with actual cabins below deck, almost-real beds, bathrooms, and even cooked food.

Everyone stayed down below in cabins except for one Milt Rackham. I was so uncomfortable in the crowded lower deck areas that I spent my entire trip above board, camped out on the deck next to PT-81 and sleeping in the unbelievably beautiful Pacific Ocean moonlight.

This farm boy from Idaho had seen the wonders of a rising moon during the weeks and weeks with livestock out on the open range, but he was unprepared for the moonlight over the Pacific Ocean. It was so bright that you could play cards and even read on deck at night.

The first light of the rising moon was breathtaking to watch as it welled up, spilled over the horizon, and blazed a trail across the dark sea to our ship. From there, it continued to ripple gently across the quiet Pacific water and etched images into my memory that would last forever. It was like molten, gently rippling glass. The wonders of God's handiwork were all about us. Indescribable.

For now, we were in the calm, peaceful eye of a hurricane called WW II that raged just over the horizon in the South Pacific. As we continued to move south, that new hurricane moved ever closer to us. Things were about to change, and here again, the change was to be beyond anything that this farm boy from Idaho could have imagined.

We spent six, sometimes eight, hours a day using flash cards to help us learn to recognize aircraft. The cards were flashed almost endlessly as we learned to bark out the nationality, type, and name of every plane that was active in the field that lay before us. If I close my eyes, I can still envision black outlines on white cards and bark the identity as fast as I can pick up and flash the cards.

"Japanese Zero . . . U.S. Marine Corsair . . . B-29 Bombed." And on and on.

As we approached the equator crossing, Skipper introduced us to his version of the two-day naval ritual of being presented before "Neptune's Court," where we had to prove our worthiness to cross the equator. The ritual involved transforming from a "slimy pollywog" to the esteemed rank of a "trusty shellback." A series of ordeals involved entertaining those who were already shellbacks by blindfolding the pollywogs and putting them through various tests of courage. For those of us who chose not to participate, Skipper privately advised us that his version was mild compared to what we would encounter on almost any other ship. Ultimately, we decided it would be wise to join in and get it over with.

I received an official certificate proving that I was now a shellback. I was told that it would guarantee a smooth ride on all future voyages across the equator. I don't recall the details, but if my 86-year-old memory serves me right, many thought our initiation into the South Pacific was enjoyable. I don't remember it as being a particularly pleasant event.

Everything came to an abrupt halt on our fifth day out. Someone heard the drone of aircraft from somewhere in the distance, and the sound of the merchant marine version of general quarters rang through the ship over the sound system. Skipper growled, "PTers! MAN, your boats!"

The message was clear. "Get off your butt and man your battle stations NOW!

You could always hear incoming planes before you could see them. Were they friends or foes? Flashcard images sprang to life in our minds as we scanned the skies and instantly recognized two Japanese Zero fighter planes making their way toward our Pacific Ocean home away from home.

We were nowhere near Japanese-occupied territory. They had no business even being where we were in the middle of the Pacific Ocean. But the combined firepower of four PT boats strapped to the deck of the lumbering merchant marine freighter dropped the planes so fast they hardly had a chance to make a decent run at us. The whole thing was over in less than 10 minutes, leaving our 50-caliber gunner spinning his turret in a 360-degree scan of the sky, disappointed that it was over so soon.

We learned later that the two Japanese fighters had launched from a Japanese aircraft carrier whose location turned out to have been a previously unknown position to U.S. military intelligence. PT-81 and its fellow squadron members were already a part of the Pacific War, and we weren't even there yet.

Meanwhile, the throb of the engines and the churning sound of the prop on the merchant marine freighter kicked up several notches from what had been a soothing, comfortable sound. We picked up speed and soon arrived in the New Hebrides Islands.

Chapter 11

Catching Up with the War in the South Pacific

We arrived at 0600 and were unloaded by 1000 hours. Our skipper called us together before lunch and told us that from now on, the fun and games were over. "From now on, it's war." He explained. "Go and get some rest, and we'll head out on our first night patrol at 2200 tonight."

The PT boats previously assigned to the South Pacific already had a proven reputation for helping the U.S. recover many of the losses at Pearl Harbor. So, despite our young age, our three squadrons from the Aleutian Islands were immediately put to work as seasoned veterans. Our welcoming ceremony amounted to no more than a brief recording of the numbers off of our dog tags, followed by our first nighttime patrol that very same night.

The South Pacific was definitely warmer than the wet, cold, windy Aleutian Islands. Still, it sounded like we were about to get involved in World War II far beyond anything that we had experienced in the North Pacific. An 18-year-old PT-81 engine mechanic named Milton Rackham didn't get much rest that evening as he watched the clock hands move toward 10 PM.

During the first nine months after our arrival at New Hebrides, the Japanese continued to have the upper hand in the war. The U.S. strategy early in the war was to at least slow Japanese advances and minimize losses while equipment, supplies, and trained military units were rapidly ramping up for a full-scale offensive move.

To us on PT-81, that meant we needed to lay low and not attract any attention from the Japanese while our war machine was hard at work. At this stage in the war, our night patrol assignments were to observe and report without letting our presence be known.

Because we could hug the shore to within a depth of only 6 feet and do so in relative silence, we were the perfect choice to engage in steath operations. We were to be the "fly on the wall" or the "mouse in the cupboard," peeking out to observe Japanese movements, capabilities, and the supply routes they were using. At one time, we had 16 squadrons of 12 PT boats each on nighttime scouting patrols with orders to observe without making contact.

This kind of work really kept us busy. In many cases, the PT boats were so overworked and worn down that we would have been hard put to last long in an all-out battle in those early months in the South Pacific.

PT-81 had been there about five months when Japanese planes did find us and came in out of the air at us. There were no Kamikaze this early in the war. Enemy planes where we were working were not particularly aggressive at first. In fact, they seemed almost wary of getting within range of our guns and would simply empty their guns in a half-hearted fly-by and then leave. It certainly wasn't because they were not capable of causing great damage. In hindsight, they were probably testing our capabilities on scouting missions similar to ours.

In other areas, air-to-sea engagement was a different story. The U.S. was taking a beating in the South Pacific; first, Pearl Harbor and now on the front lines in New Guinea, where briefings indicated that they were sinking *nine out of every eleven* of our supply ships.

The Japanese fighter planes were the best in the world at the beginning of WW II. Their planes featured a very strong, well-engineered fuselage capable of both high maneuverability at slow speed and high speed at long range. Heavier, slower U.S. aircraft were outclassed by Japanese fighter planes and could not survive one-on-one battles in the sky.

As in the Aleutians, if it had not been for good old Yankee ingenuity, things could have been a lot worse. U.S. pilots realized that they needed to come up with a strategy that gave them an advantage, and it wasn't long before they developed a survival strategy that worked.

U.S Pilots found that they could fly higher than the Japanese planes and soon adopted a "dive, slash, and run" approach. They would fly in at high elevations, locate Japanese fighters who could not reach them, and then dive down through an enemy formation with as much firepower as they could carry. They would then use the speed they had attained to rise up and out of reach, usually before Japanese fighters could retaliate. The strategy enabled them to survive against the Japanese during the time it took to design and build improved U.S. planes.

One shortcut in engineering is to capture a working example of a successful design and gain insights that save time in developing new designs. The U.S. worked hard to capture an intact, fully flyable Japanese Zero with only partial success. The answer finally came in the Aleutians when a Japanese Zero, returning from a raid on Dutch Harbor, ran out of gas after downing a U.S. plane.

His mistake came when he went back to take the time and fuel to strafe the U.S. survivors in the ocean. The Japanese pilot, accompanied by two others, came in for a landing on what appeared to be a grass-covered field. In actuality, it was a tundra-covered area pocketed with pot-holes of water. The plane hit the tundra, flipped forward, and landed upside down with only a minimum amount of damage.

The accompanying Japanese planes had orders to destroy the downed plane but couldn't bring themselves to do it without knowing if the pilot had survived. In the process, they left the plane behind, where it fell into American hands.

Meanwhile, back in the South Pacific, our PT boat squadrons continued our regular patrols, covertly assisting military intelligence in piecing together knowledge of Japanese movements. We were initially instructed not to engage the enemy in any way that would cause them to discover that we were building up our military strength in preparation for major offensives. This included safeguarding the secret that a steady buildup of PT boat squadrons was underway and set to be much more lethal in the coming months.

Those were very busy months for us. We left base to gather intelligence between 1000 and 1200 and returned around 600 hours on a schedule that often ran for weeks at a time without a break.

Chapter 12

PT Boats Did Not Come With Luxury Accommodations

PT boats not only came without luxury accommodations, but they also came without some things you might consider to be bare necessities, such as bathrooms. I need to explain how the lack of a bathroom is handled on a PT boat in order to set the stage for the rest of this chapter.

Let me caution readers to read carefully for the next couple of paragraphs because I am only going to go through this one time.

The term "poop deck" is a nautical term NOT used to describe any part of a PT boat officially. But, with a little imagination, it does create a mental image that explains why you might see a crewman carrying an empty pail toward the stern.

At the stern, there is a small, comfortable, open-air, relatively private space between the torpedo and the depth charges located on either side of the boat. We called it the "poop deck". Rather than discuss definitions you may find on the internet, let's just agree that I have taken a literary license and move on.

A crewman who needs to do some business also needs water in his pail. When you are moving at 45 miles per hour, the only safe place to collect a bucket of seawater for your trip to the PT bathroom is at the stern of the boat. As the boat cuts through the water, it creates a thin, bow-like wave that travels the complete length of the boat and rises into the air at the stern. At those speeds, the wave sprays as if coming out of a fire hose with tremendous force. The stream of water is within arm's reach of a crewman. If he leans carefully over the edge of the boat, he can dip his pail into the stream of water. Care and judgment are critical, however, since too deep a dip into the high-velocity stream can pull both the pail and the crewman off the boat and into the sea, something that does happen now and then.

You might first envision the pail being used in place of a toilet seat, but I can testify that it is NOT a good idea to try to sit on a pail full of salt water while riding on a PT boat at 45 miles per hour in the open sea. No, you don't sit on the pail; you first seat yourself between the torpedo and the depth charge and then use the pail as a flushing system to clean off the deck.

Okay, okay. If you haven't quite got the picture yet, just forget about it, and let's move on. Stick with me. The above description of collecting a pail of seawater on your way to a PT boat bathroom is critical. It sets the stage for the rest of this story, which is an important part of my PT boat experience.

As the intensity of the war increased all around us, we saw less and less of our skipper. A more formal "officer-crew" relationship developed to replace what we realized had probably been too much of a causal relationship up to then.

One day, a new, freshly graduated replacement for one of the increasing number of fallen PT-81 crewmembers arrived. We were surprised and somewhat defensive when he asked us what it felt like to be assigned to serve under a "glory hound."

In the ensuing conversation, it turned out that we were the last to know about what was happening in our own PT boat family, much as is often the case in what was once a happy relationship. The PT boat neighborhood had been talking about our skipper for some time. Now that we were alert to what everybody else already knew, we did start to notice glory hound behavior.

Our levels of intensity never faltered while battling the enemy, but in our quiet times between battles, the words commonly used in some circles to describe wooden hulled PT boats as being "expendable" took on new meaning. As the pressures of an escalating war increased, Skipper began to "tighten the reins" and really push PT-81 and its crew to the limit. He was frequently unreasonable in his expectations, constantly sniffing around, finding, and then volunteering us for more high-risk special assignments than was normal.

We had become "expendable" now, as it was clear that the addition of new "line items" on Skipper's resume had become more important to him than anything else, including the safety of his crew. One night, early into a patrol, someone asked if anyone had seen Skipper. After a thorough search, we realized that he was no longer on board. We discussed what to do next and decided to continue the mission and figure out what to do on the way back to base as far as reporting our loss.

As we headed back, we spotted Skipper bobbing up and down in the Pacific Ocean, securely wrapped in his life vest in the now-rising sun. We circled the boat and picked up a very angry, salt water-soaked Skipper who began threatening the entire crew with court martial even before his foot touched the rescue ladder.

Court martial charges were filed against us, and each of us was called in for pre-trial questioning. No one knew what had happened, although more than half the crew did testify that they had seen Skipper lose the bathroom pail on more than one occasion while dipping in the spray at the stern and that he had been observed to have been nearly pulled overboard more than once.

The court-martial charges were dropped. But trouble for Skipper and for PT-81 was just beginning.

Chapter 13

Picking Up Military Intelligence and an Engine Full of Sand

It was a dark, moonless night as we gathered with Skipper to receive our usual briefing for the night patrol. He talked to us for a couple of minutes and announced that it was time to go. We looked at each other, wondering what was going on. He hadn't told us anything about our mission.

We arrived at our assigned position, and Skipper throttled back in mid-ocean. PT-81 settled, low and silent, into the water. He pulled us together in the chart house and filled us in on our share of the details of our assignment.

We were to rig for silent running for the remaining miles to our pickup point. Silent running meant moving at a slow speed with steel baffles dropped down over the engine exhausts so that the exhaust would be discharged underwater to deaden the sound. We were entering enemy territory and, as always, wanted to avoid detection.

We slowly approached an island that was barely visible in the dark night and entered a bay. Skipper gave a single light flash to announce his presence and then maneuvered away just in case the Japanese were also on shore waiting for us to identify our location so they could fire on us.

Skipper waited quietly. There was no sound anywhere. It felt like even the jungle was holding its breath. All we knew was that we were going to pick someone up, so we continued to wait, more anxiously as minutes passed, without saying a word.

This was our first time for this kind of drama, and it felt like we were in the movies. Just as we started to breathe normally, we were aware of a slight rock in the boat and turned to see a wet, shiny-black figure slither up and over the edge at the stern. The first impression was that it wouldn't be too difficult to think that it was a mermaid or something. But the mirage became a reality as our skipper came forward without a word and silently escorted our guest to the chart house. After several minutes, Skipper motioned for the closest man to join them.

Whisperings were exchanged, and we were informed that we were silently moving this U.S. Navy SEAL to a new location on another island. Once back on the open sea, our passenger joined the crew, with his skin-tight rubber suit now loosened and his cap removed.

He was friendly and easy to talk to. Our crew stood around him, fascinated by this image of war that had suddenly appeared out of the dark jungle for transportation to another dot on the map. I remember that we all had questions about food, supplies, and a weapon and how he could have gotten on our boat before we even knew he was there.

After 66 years, the details of his answers are blurred, but the flavor of the conversation is still vivid. He explained that he was not entirely alone and that there were small caches of supplies well hidden in the jungle. He also explained that the Japanese had supplies that were always available in an emergency and that they had never yet even noticed that there might be a little here and a little there that might disappear now and then.

As far as a weapon, he motioned to a lump in his rubber suit that hardly seemed big enough to be a weapon of any significance. He explained that sneaking on and off a boat in the dark without being seen was what he was trained to do and that he could hide behind a tuft of grass if his life depended on it.

Time passed swiftly, and we soon arrived at our destination. We crept silently into a South Pacific Bay that looked like all the others and watched without blinking so that we wouldn't miss the disappearance of our first Navy SEAL.

World War II had a wide range of impacts on those who were involved that varied all over the map. For many, like our first Navy SEAL, the war honed them into levels of performance that included heroism, leadership, high skill, decency, and professionalism. But for a few at the other end of the spectrum, the war developed character traits in men that ranged from being a royal pain in the neck to being an outright danger to those around them.

I had originally intended not to cover this topic, but it has become apparent to me now that my story would not be complete without it. The PT-81 skipper who started out with us when we left for our Aleutian assignment was a man with the skills and enthusiasm required to do his job and do it well. PT-81 became a team of 18-year-olds that had learned to perform above and beyond the call of duty on more than one occasion, something that continued well into our South Pacific assignment.

Then, under Skipper's command, PT-81 began to occasionally "take the long way home", picking up dangerous additional assignments on our way back to base after an all-night patrol. It wasn't uncommon, for example, for Skipper to order us into an exploration of hidden waterways and very dangerous inland areas that were well outside the areas we had been assigned. Our now-Glory-Hound Skipper's methods ended up putting us in an increasing number of Japanese encounters and fire-fights that were beginning to take a disproportionate toll on our crew. Our body count started to rise well beyond what was normal or expected.

Clandestine operations of picking up and dropping men (like Navy SEALs) and information pouches continued, but they did not always run as smoothly as our first one. On one occasion, after going through the ritual of silent running, arrival, and signaling our presence, Skipper ordered us to abandon our normal protocols and approach the dangerous shoreline instead of waiting out of range, as usual, to be boarded.

We anchored PT-81 at a point that had been marked by a coded light signal and watched as our glory hound skipper dropped over the side of the boat, himself, into the water. He disappeared into the dark jungle canopy with a canvas Navy intelligence pouch strapped over his shoulder. His orders to us were to wait for his return with absolutely no noise and required speaking only in a low whisper.

I went below deck to check the engines.

After ten minutes with the engines, I returned top side and sensed that we had drifted. I went to Shoe, a young crewman nicknamed for his size 14 shoes, and told him we were drifting toward shore. Shoe looked around, shrugged his shoulders, and whispered, "No way!"

I watched for the next thirty seconds and confirmed that we WERE drifting slowly backward in water that was now approaching six feet deep, the point at which our boat would begin to drag bottom and could become beached in enemy territory.

I looked at Shoe and whispered, "Yes, we are!"

Just then, the skipper appeared out of the thick jungle along the beach. He stared at us and whispered, "You're drifting!" as he started to wade toward us through the water. He was halfway to us when one of the three propellers dug into the sand with a scraping sound, and the boat quivered to a stop.

The sea gently rocked the boat, which slowly embedded itself, first propellers and then exhaust baffles, solidly into the sand in enemy territory. As we tried to push, pull, and rock the 80-foot boat free, the slight waves from offshore steadily drove it deeper into the sand. Shoe even dove underwater with a steel plate and tried to shovel, pull, and scrape us free, but to no avail.

Now sitting ducks, we ended up radioing for help in an area where there could have been Japanese camped anywhere along the shoreline or in the jungle. Another PT boat was then put in harm's way to rescue us, and within minutes, we were free and headed for home . . . at the end of a tow line.

Sand had been forced up into the exhaust pipe and packed so tightly that the engines would not even start. I could tell that Skipper was furious about what had happened. He started to question me but found that he couldn't continue. We all stayed out of his way for the trip home.

We could all tell that this incident wasn't over, and we wondered how it was going to play out.

Chapter 14

War is a Fiery Furnace that Forges the Character of Men

The War had no mercy on those who fought to preserve this country. There were those who were killed and those who survived in what seemed to be some sort of endless, random selection process. For those who survived, the War forged the character of men and women with levels of citizenship, appreciation for the country, and a belief in a set of values and principles that contributed to a growing America.

The fiery furnace of war also transformed initially good, sound men into men corrupted to the point that their behavior became troublesome and then intolerable. The lives of men were at stake. In the days that followed our near disaster with the intelligence pouch, things on PT-81 deteriorated rapidly, culminating in a confrontation between Skipper and myself that brought things to a head.

As the boat's engine mechanic, I was officially in charge of several crew members who were working to remove the sand from the engine exhaust systems on each of our three 16-cylinder Packard engines. We had one engine almost ready to test start, with the other two still torn down and inoperative. Skipper arrived, found that we had one of three engines ready to test, and ordered us to start it up and prepare for a special mission.

I spoke up, saying that the boat would not survive a battle situation with only one engine and that I still did not have confidence that even that one was ready. Skipper stiffened, and the crew pulled back.

He faced me, addressed me using my official rank as the official U.S. Power Torpedo Boat #81 Engine Mechanic, thrust a clipboard in my face, and ordered me to sign off that the engine was ready.

I refused to sign.

After further grilling and my second and then third refusal, Skipper called the MPs. I was charged with insubordination and spent my first and only night in the brig.

The base commanding officer called me into his office the next morning. He asked what I was doing in the brig and questioned me thoroughly. He noted that my record was spotless and rose from behind his desk. He walked with me back toward PT-81, where we found several of my crew members working on the second and third engines.

The C.O. gathered our skipper, along with the rest of the crew, and began questioning each crewman working on the boat's engines. He was interrupted by the skipper several times, who silenced him with a hand motion as he continued to get to the bottom of the situation. The grilling went something like this:

"Do you have engine number one up and running?"

"Yes, Sir!"

"Was it running yesterday?"

No, Sir!"

"Are either of the other two engines ready to run?"

"No, SIR!"

"Is this boat safe to run with only one engine?"

"No, Sir!"

"Can this boat maneuver in a battle with one engine?"

"No, Sir!"

"Would these two other engines operate if you put them back together right now?"

"Absolutely not, Sir!"

"Do you know what you're doing here?"

"Oh, YES, Sir!"

At the end of the questioning, the base commanding officer turned and escorted our skipper back to his office. When Skipper came back, he never said a word to any of us the rest of the day. We later heard through the Navy grapevine that the C.O. had read him the riot act. The skipper who had gotten us safely through the Battle of Attu had been told that he had one of the best PT crews in the entire Navy and that, if he couldn't handle it, there was a kitchen duty job waiting for him that would keep him busy for the rest of the war.

In spite of everything, things went from bad to worse over the next few weeks. I requested another meeting with the base commanding officer to file a request for transfer. He leaned over his desk, looked me right in the eye, and asked, "Is it really that bad over there?" I never moved a muscle as I looked back and quietly said, "Yes, Sir."

I passed Skipper on his way to the C.O.'s office as I walked back to PT-81. Skipper returned within half an hour, packed his bags, and left without saying a word to anyone.

We met our new skipper two days later. He proved to be a man who was much like the skipper we started out with in the Aleutians, but he never lost his focus on why he was on board PT-81. He knew he was there to provide the leadership required to protect our country and our families back home *and* to do everything he could to get us all back home as soon as possible so we could carry on with the rest of our lives.

In the beginning, we weren't sure how to treat him, but he broke the ice by making the first move. The South Pacific is a warm place to be with beautiful, clear, blue Pacific Ocean water as far as you can see. There is water, water, everywhere, but not a drop that is drinkable or conducive to a freshwater shower. Let me tell you; there comes a time when you dream of a freshwater shower or a swim in fresh water to get really clean and to sometimes just cool off. A few days after our new skipper came aboard, we were standing in the heat looking out across the ocean when he asked, "How far away do you think that is?"

We all looked up, expecting to see something special, but couldn't see anything unusual. Squinting now at the horizon, he repeated the question. "Those storm clouds there, with all that fresh rain pouring into the ocean. How far away do you think they are from here?"

We looked back and recognized what he was talking about. Within the next hour, and without much more than a word or two, we had filled our 3,000-gallon fuel tanks, checked the engine oil, checked our soap, towel, and extra ration supply, and signed out for a daytime patrol.

We were all giddy, just like the bunch of 19-year-old boys we were. We ended up having to wait a while before we left. Half the crew had almost forgotten that they had run out of their month's supply of their favorite brew-ski brand and had to go back to camp and barter for several cases. When they finally arrived, we were on our way to find out how far we were from a cool, refreshing rain shower.

After a two-hour trip out, two unforgettable hours in the rain, and a two-hour trip back to get to know our new skipper, we were relieved to give him our stamp of approval. We rested up for our nightly patrol and settled back into our routine, concentrating only on the Japanese as our enemy and happy to be free of interruptions and distractions that had nothing to do with winning the war.

The above memory reminds me of other pleasant incidents that were enhanced because they occurred in wartime situations, sometimes even within the sound of gunfire. There were volunteers—celebrities who risked their lives to visit troops in the field. Bob Hope stands out in my mind, as does Dorothy Lamoure. Mr. Hope had the audience in the palm of his hand from the moment he appeared from behind whatever we had available as a curtain. He spent more holidays with the troops than he spent at home.

He and all the others who came to honor and entertain us were never, ever forgotten. Those of us on the PT boat crews were fortunate. We were often called upon to shuttle them from place to place, which gave us a unique opportunity to spend time with them one-on-one. Mr. Hope was especially friendly and easy to talk to.

On three different occasions, we rearranged our schedules by a few hours to see Bob Hope perform. He was really worth seeing . . . a real boost to those of us who were in the middle of the war. Another favorite was Errol Flynn. We saw him up in the Aleutian Islands.

It's hard to explain how much it meant to the troops to have these folks risk their lives to come to us out in the war zones. It felt like a message from home.

Chapter 15

If It's the Right Thing to Do, The Lord Knows How to Do It

Speaking of connections to home, there is one wartime memory that, for me, stands out head and shoulders above them all.

Each PT base had a supply ship that was most precious to them. We called them our motherships because they were our connections to the things that kept us alive: good food, ammunition, spare parts, and clothing, and a few things that helped make life bearable, like beer, cigarettes, and letters and packages from home.

We returned to base one day and found our mothership sitting on the bottom of the Pacific Ocean. She was sticking up out of about 30 feet of water after having been hit by a Japanese Kamikaze. Within days, Navy divers repaired the damage below her waterline using underwater welding techniques I never knew existed. Pumps were then used to empty her hull, and we all watched as she slowly rose from her watery grave.

It was not unusual to utilize PT crews for a variety of tasks during a portion of the daytime hours between our nighttime patrols, so we were not surprised when our skipper announced that we had been assigned to clean the supply ship. We were surprised, however, when we discovered that, in this case, "clean the ship" meant to gather, identify, tag, and remove the remains of 250 Navy crewmen who had been on board when she went down.

Frank Eugene McKuster and I were the first two to go aboard and below deck to start the work. We picked our way through level after level of twisted metal and finally made our way down to the bottom. We filled our first basket in about 30 minutes and made our way back up to the top deck for some much-needed fresh air.

I can hardly describe how bad it was. Just filling baskets with gathered dog tags and torn, charred, and scattered remains would have been bad enough all by itself, but that wasn't the biggest problem. The ship had been sitting in the blistering South Pacific sun for a week and a half, and the air below deck was hot, humid, and reeked of the terrible stench of death and decay. The odor was almost more than you could stand.

After recovering in the fresh air, Eugene told me that he didn't know what I was going to do, but he wasn't going back down there. "They can kill me or throw me in the brig or whatever they want." He said. "But I just *cannot* do that again."

Meanwhile, word got around about how bad the cleanup detail was, and nobody was eager to have any part of it. I continued to go back and forth by myself and managed to fill four more baskets before Skipper came up and told me it was time to quit. He called us together and said to get some rest before the evening patrol; the base commander would meet with us the next day.

The base commander gathered us and went through our squadron, giving each man a chance to say what he thought about the assignment. I was the last one, and before I could speak, the commander asked me if I could put together a team of men who would work with me to get the job done.

I must have turned as white as a sheet. I had never been able to handle the tight spaces below the deck of *any* ship. I had stayed on deck next to PT-81 during the entire trip from Seattle to New Hebrides rather than sleep in the cramped, claustrophobic cabins on the merchant marine ship. And now, to perform the task of gathering human remains from such a place seemed completely unthinkable.

I finally spoke up and told the commander that I didn't know if I could do it. The commander asked me what I would need to try and told me he would arrange whatever I needed regarding supplies. He also said that he wouldn't force me or anyone else to do it but that it did need to be done. I asked him if I could have some time to myself, and he dismissed the men, walked out, shut the door, and left me alone in his private quarters.

I finally came out the door. In the time that I had spent alone, I had been reminded of advice I had received years earlier: that prayer should be a two-way conversation, with at least as much time spent in quiet listening as in prayerful gratitude, pleading, and requests for direction.

I prayed earnestly about the assignment there in the C.O.'s private quarters. And then I listened. I came away with a sure knowledge that those who had perished in our mothership were precious in the eyes of the Lord. They were precious in the hearts of their family members and in the hearts of all the men they had supplied in this theater of operations. I knew they deserved to be respected, gathered, identified, and sent home for closure if it was at all humanly possible to do so.

As far as my anxiety about being asked to do the job, I was assured that I would not be alone in the work, and I surely wasn't. I experienced an awareness of a spiritual kind of support that stayed with me through the entire ordeal. It helped me with a special kind of discernment as I gathered and packaged what was left of the ship's crew.

I worked alone for over a week when a PT crewman began approaching me with questions about what it was that enabled me to go back into that ship each day. I tried to explain what I believed to be true, that if we ask and then listen, the Lord will help us discern what it is that we need to do. And that if something was the right thing to do, then the Lord knew how to do it and would show us how, if we asked.

Two crew members joined me on the cleaning detail for a short time after that, and when one of those two men quit, the work continued with only myself and one other crew member, one Frank Eugene Mc Kuster. That same man who had started the job with me and quit after the first 30 minutes came back to finish the job with me so that I wouldn't have to do it alone.

You don't meet many men like Frank Eugene Mc Kuster during your lifetime. When Eugene first came to me after he quit the first time, he and I talked about the project in our barracks for two hours one night. I tried to explain to why I just had to get the job done. I asked him if he was one of those men down there in that hold, would he want to be just left there without at least a dog tag or something to send back home? If you were a mother or father or someone else who took care of your boy, raised him and loved him, wouldn't you want a dog tag or something to cherish in memory of your son?

Before he left, Eugene told me he could see how I felt and understood why I had to continue. He told me that he couldn't stand by and let me do it alone, that he would work with me if we could just have a prayer before we went down each day.

After our discussion, Eugene sat quietly for a few minutes before getting up to leave. He paused uncertainly and said, "Also, Milt, I notice you every night at the bow of the boat before we go out on patrol. I've been wanting to ask you about it."

He paused again to gather his thoughts. "Part of the reason I came here tonight was to get up enough courage to help you with cleaning the ship. Because I figure if I can help you with this job, I can feel worthy enough to ask you if I could join you at the bow each night. I'd like to be a part of your prayer before we leave on night patrol, Milt. Would that be okay with you?"

I looked up, hot tears in my eyes, and told him that he was more than welcome to join me at the bow of the boat and that I needed all the help I could get.

We stood, shook hands, and parted.

Chapter 16

Time at the Bow of the Boat Before Night-Time Patrols

PT boats regularly went out on dangerous, clandestine nighttime patrols. We left base between 10 PM and midnight and returned around 6 AM on a schedule that often had us running from island to island for weeks at a time without a break. We never knew what to expect or if those who left with us each night would make it back alive in the morning.

I had been in the habit of spending some time alone in prayer at the bow of the boat each evening before heading out on patrol. The rest of the crew would be on the dock or in the back of the boat before a patrol, so the bow was usually a quiet place to pray for the mission, the safety of the crew, and, as the boat mechanic, for the boat itself.

One evening, I noticed a couple of crewmen standing quietly off to one side. They began coming back each night. One of them was Frank Eugene Mc Kuster, and when he and I talked about it, he welcomed the invitation to join me at the bow.

He mentioned that he and several others had talked about it and had wondered if they could be a part of my nighttime prayers. In the days that followed, other members of the crew would show up at the bow in the evening, and before you knew it, the whole crew was there every night, including our new skipper.

At first, the prayer was more of a "moment of silence," but one day, Skipper called me in and asked if I could pray aloud during meetings, and it became a part of PT-81 from that time on. We worked together as a team in everything we did, including seeking Heavenly assistance in the protection of our country, a timely end to the war, and the preservation of our very lives.

Prayer before nighttime patrol was not the only occasion for prayer by any means. One particular example was the three days and two nights I spent floating in the Pacific Ocean with two of my crewmates.

It all started one night while we were on patrol. As we rounded a point of land on an island, we came into the path of a Japanese destroyer who saw us first. We were under fire before we even knew he was there. Skipper quickly executed evasive maneuvers with a high-speed turn, releasing a dense black smoke screen to conceal our location. It all happened so fast that three of us couldn't grab hold of anything fast enough, and we were thrown overboard.

Skipper paused, and we waved him on, knowing that we would be safer in the water if the destroyer didn't see him trying to rescue us as the smoke screen began to clear. Within minutes, both the Japanese destroyer and our PT boat were out of sight, and the three of us were left alone in the middle of the ocean.

It was after midnight when we went overboard and we spent two nights and three days floating there. The sun was viciously hot, and the risk of sunburn and sunstroke was real. Two of us used our shorts during the day to cover our heads and shoulders and at night to catch condensation as our only source of drinking water. It's amazing how much fresh water you can suck out of a freshly "dew-moistened" pair of shorts when you are dying of thirst while floating in the middle of water as far as you can see in every direction.

One of our group of three wouldn't listen to us and didn't take his shorts off to protect his upper body or to gather fresh water. By the second day, he had swallowed sea water instead and had begun to hallucinate. We tried to restrain him as he fought to free himself to swim towards rescuers that he envisioned walking on the water.

When he recognized his own father as one of the imagined rescuers, he became so violent that we could not hold him, and he began to swim away. We tried to catch him as he violently fought his way through the water, calling out to his father. He removed his life jacket so he could swim more easily and then slipped into the depths before we could get to him.

In the next day and night, we saw a Japanese Destroyer and a Japanese cruiser, who luckily did not see us, and several of our own search planes. At the end of the third day, we recognized PT 98 in the distance and caught their attention by yelling and waving our precious, life-preserving shorts. They had gotten ahold of some ocean current information and were crisscrossing the ocean to find us.

Once on shore, we discovered how weak we were. Our arms and legs were uncoordinated, along with the rest of us. The base commander was on the dock to greet us and see if we were all right. Once he determined that we would be okay, I heard him talking to the head cook about some of that "really good" beef stew. We were soon in the mess hall with a bowl of warmed-up stew. It was the best meal, the very best beef stew that I have ever had in my life.

As my thoughts for this chapter about prayer began to pull together, I was drawn again to the notion that "If it's the right thing to do, the Lord knows how to do it." I have begun to wonder if there is something there for me regarding at least one of the reasons why I'm writing this book in the first place.

I have been praying earnestly every single night since I decided to write this book, hoping that sharing my story will free me from my nightmares. However, I am beginning to wonder about a few things. What if the relief I need is really beyond what I can do for myself? What if my healing will only come when my experiences become useful to someone else who needs to know that *they* are not alone? The right thing for me, at this point in my life, may very well be to connect with and help others who are also dealing with the lasting effects of traumatic wartime experiences trapped inside them.

Just thinking about this quiets me. The doors of my memory are now wide open, and I am recording everything that comes to my mind as calmly as I can. It's as if I am inviting these dreams to come out in the open without knowing what to do with them beyond helping get them onto a printed page.

I trust that the Lord and my writer will know what to do from there.

As I have gone through this process, my dreams have escalated again: two, sometimes three, a week. But this work is certainly about more than just me. There are those who have offered to expand the sound of my voice and extend the reach of my pen. That assistance has come out of the clear blue sky, and that fact, in itself, testifies to me that sharing my story is the right thing to do.

For me, the right thing to do has always been to place myself in the hands of the Lord. I accept the will of the Lord, whether or not it brings an end to my dreams, if it will help someone else to heal.

From now on, I will do all that I can do and leave the rest to Him. This new understanding has made what was once the hardest thing I have ever done take on a whole new light and meaning.

Chapter 17

PT Night Patrol in the Company of Unexpected Guests

We are on night patrol again, this time looking for Japanese supply barges. In the early years of the war, they used larger ships to transport supplies, but as the war has progressed and American forces have gained steam, the Japanese have been incurring heavy losses to their supply transports.

Because of this, they have begun using smaller barges and even Sampans to minimize those losses. We PT boats have the advantage in speed, maneuverability, and firepower that allows us to take out any supply vessel, regardless of size.

The shipping lanes between the islands of the South Pacific became known as "Tin Can Alleys," because the bottom of the ocean along those passages became littered with Japanese and American ships of all sizes as the war dragged on. Looking for Japanese supply barges meant sitting and waiting for them to appear in those narrow channels. When we were assigned to intercept the supply ships, our job was to hunker and stalk for hours of patient waiting, followed by a burst of activity, to sink a supply ship and its escorts, and then move to a new location where we would return to silent hunkering.

You never ever stayed put after revealing your location unless you wanted to be there when the Japanese bombers came by to take you out of action. There were some times, of course, when you ended up having to go back to base camp for repairs or to get a wounded crewman to help in a hurry. There were also rare occasions when you sent a May Day for a tow rope.

PT-81 had its full share of all of the above.

On this particular night, we had quietly entered a bay that had an open view of the supply lanes. We were in predatory hunker mode. I had been below with the engines, checking the mufflers that were extended over the exhaust pipes and into the water to silence the three Packard engines that idled in constant readiness.

All was well as I walked quietly toward the chart house. I listened to the slow, muffled, barely audible "Uba . . . uba . . . uba . . . uba" sound of the idling engines. It always amazed me how well that sound blended so easily into the natural sounds of the night.

As I neared the chart house, I suddenly paused and felt the hair on the back of my neck stiffen. This was something that might happen if you were suddenly startled by a sound or if there was a sudden cold draft. But the South Pacific night was full of nothing more than natural sounds, and the air was warm and comfortable.

I stopped and tried to put my finger on what was bothering me. You soon learn to do that when you live in constant danger within a war zone. You carry that instinct with you for the rest of the war and, for that matter, the rest of your life. But more about that later.

I stopped and began to wonder if we were alone out there on the open water. I stood quietly to let my eyes get used to the darkness and then slowly scanned the water around PT-81. I strained my eyes for the long, low outline of a Japanese supply barge. There was nothing but black water against an even blacker sky. I had begun a second, even slower scan when I something inside me began questioning why I was looking only for the outline of a small Japanese barge.

Almost immediately, I began to see the outline of a large ship. A very, very large ship, ten or more times longer than our

80-foot PT boat. It was sitting parallel to us, portside, some 500 yards away.

Was my mind playing tricks on me? I didn't wait for an answer and continued my now very quiet steps toward the chart house, where I found Skipper sitting not so patiently, staring into the darkness. He looked up when I came in, and I pointed and mouthed the word, "Look…"

He raised his binoculars toward my pointing finger and slowly scanned the darkness. I heard a faintly whispered, "Uh-oh…" Then, as he continued his binocular probe in a 360-degree sweep toward starboard, I saw him stiffen.

He leaned toward me and whispered, "Jap Destroyers. Two of 'em, one each side! 500 yards. Crew on guns. Torpedos stand by. And, tell our boys to hang onto their shorts 'cause when we leave, it's gonna be in a big hurry!"

In the moments that followed, there were muffled footsteps on our wooden deck as we all moved into position. Just as I got behind my 37 mm at bow position, the silence of the night was ripped wide open. The sound of ringing bells and sirens on first one and then both Japanese ships signaled general quarters, and all Japanese hands rushed to battle-ready positions.

A spotlight on the bow side of one of the destroyers flashed on and locked a glaring, targeting beam right on us. It blinded us for just an instant before one of our crack-shot 50 caliber machine gunners squeezed a round that shattered the light 500 yards away and re-darkened the night. (The 50 calibers were effective up to a mile, and at 500 yards, they were deadly in the hands of a crack shot.)

Both destroyers now flashed spotlights in our direction as our machine gunners took turns popping out spotlights as fast as they came on. It was as if these young kids were at the turkey shoot booth at the Idaho State Fair, showing off for their girlfriends.

But this was life and death, not a turkey shoot. All of our guns now arched tracer bullets into the sky as we poured everything we had into both Japanese destroyers to keep them as distracted as possible from their goal of sinking us.

We could just make out their big guns spinning in our direction when I heard Skipper say, "I can hardly believe this!

It looks like those two ships are going to take a shot at us! Don't they realize that they'll be shooting at EACH OTHER?"

Everything happened at once after that. Just as Skipper hammered the throttle and 3600 HP threw us forward, up, and out of the water, both Japanese ships flashed fire, smoke, and live ammo from their guns. We all hung on to the still-accelerating PT boat as we strained to look back to see if any of the destroyers' shells actually did hit each other in friendly fire, but all we could see was the black sea against a black, moonless sky.

The enemy no doubt thought that they had caught us in the process of sneaking up on them. Little did they know that we were just as surprised as they were that we had all been sharing the same lagoon as a parking lot while we waited for targets to pass by in the night.

Our surprise encounter with the two Japanese destroyers was not our only intimate moment with the enemy. On another night, in another island bay, we had arrived in silent mode and were waiting quietly after having signaled our arrival with a flash of lights. We were all watching the jungle shoreline intently when one of us asked, "What is that? Over there . . . in the water."

All we could see was a ripple traveling behind what looked like the big ugly head of a sea snake sticking out of the water while the rest of its body was moving past us beneath the surface. Skipper turned to look and whispered, "It's a Japanese submarine . . . silent running . . . periscope depth."

We didn't move or make a sound as the sub quietly slipped past us. As soon as it had completely entered the bay, the skipper gave the word to get our depth charges ready. We moved into position over the deep entry channel, and we came to life. We launched precision depth charges to explode at different depths, and soon, there was a hint of an oil slick, indicating damage to the sub below. We didn't want to be a welcoming committee to whatever Japanese assistance might be on the way, so we fired up and left the area with 3600 HP pushing us up, up, and away. The Navy later entered the bay with divers and confirmed that we had destroyed a Japanese submarine and, presumably, all 90-plus souls on board.

Chapter 18
PT Boats Used as Troop Landing Craft

The United States continued to build military strength in the South Pacific and reached the point where it could press attacks and retake islands that had previously been lost to the Japanese. As the tide of war turned in favor of the U.S., General MacArthur fulfilled his pledge, and he did return to the Philippines. He came back the same way he left, by PT boat, and landed at Tacloban, Leyte, on 24 October 1944.

The tide of the South Pacific War turned in favor of America and General MacArthur fulfilled his pledge to return to the Pacific Theater. He came back the way he left; by PT boat.

The U.S. accelerated its advancement toward the Japanese homeland using a "capture and kill" approach. Our strategy involved capturing every other island, which would then leave pockets of Japanese troops stranded on islands that were surrounded by U.S. military forces and heavily armed PT boats on four sides.

PT boats patrolled the water between the islands to cut Japanese supply lines and keep the stranded soldiers trapped with dwindling supplies of food, ammunition, medicine, and Saki. At one time, PT-81 and RON-13, a squadron of 11 other PT boats, were responsible for holding 42,000 Japanese troops in isolation on these islands scattered for miles across the South Pacific.

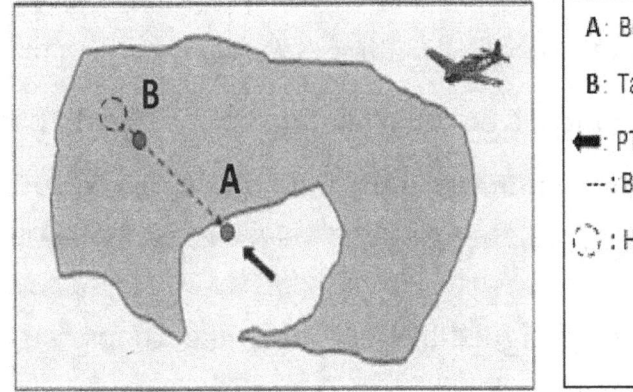

The battles became increasingly intense as the enemy's defenses stiffened at the realization that the U.S. was moving toward their homeland. Japanese resistance on the landing beaches became so severe that U.S. planners decided to include PT boats in carrying troops ashore alongside the regular landing craft.

Landing craft vessels were designed with special ramps that permitted a direct approach to the beaches and a quick discharge of troops. Still, they did not have the firepower to cover the troops during the delivery process. They discharged their load of troops and retreated.

Although PT boats had far less capacity to carry troops, had no landing ramp, and could approach a beach to only a six-foot depth, we did have the advantage of *massive* firepower. A PT boat could deploy troops over the side in six feet of water and then remain in position to provide cover as they made their way toward the ground cover beyond the open beach area. The disadvantage of using the PT boat for landing troops was that they required special attention to get them as near to the beach as possible without beaching themselves.

When PT-81 was assigned the job of landing troops, we followed a process that began with the use of our massive firepower as soon as we were within range of the landing area.

We fired blindly at first and then at gun and mortar flashes from the enemy's return fire. PT-81 had a six-foot draft, which meant that we could advance toward the beach until the boat hull touched the bottom at a water depth of six feet.

These were the days before sonar or radar. This meant that carefully measuring water depth during a beach landing fell to a crew member sprawled at the bow "sounding" or checking the depth with a measuring chain and calling it out to the skipper.

I can still hear it in my memory. Amid the sound of constant firing and the "rub, dub, dub" of the idling engine, you would hear, "12 feet, Sir . . . 10 feet, Sir . . . 8 feet, Sir . . . 7 feet, Sir . . . 6 feet . . . and   . . . CONTACT!" as the skipper slowly throttled back and then gently bumped the beach bottom.

While we eased them in, the landing troops sat ready on board, their rifle barrels capped with waterproof plugs. They dropped over the side into water over their head and moved quickly toward shore to get their heads and rifle barrels above water. At a three-foot depth, they uncapped their rifles and commenced firing.

The PT boat stayed in position and continued to provide a blanket of machine gun fire that proved to be very effective in preventing the enemy from enjoying free target practice on our troops. The use of PT boats as landing craft forced the Japanese defensive line farther back from the beach, which was a welcome relief to soldiers struggling for their first foothold.

Before long, the Japanese introduced a new twist to their beach defense by placing snipers in trees along the beach area. They had orders to hold their fire until our landing troops had passed their position. As they began picking off our boys from behind, our PT boats quickly learned to concentrate our firepower on the sniper positions. The sniper either fell out of the tree, or the tree itself would be reduced to a skeleton that then revealed what was left of the sniper, still strapped in its branches.

As you might imagine, the banter between Army and Navy personnel during off-duty time included a variety of comments and comebacks. One of my favorites was the comparison between Navy PT boats and Army landing craft.

Army: "Aw, come ON! PT boats are used as landing craft because they are *expendable*."

NAVY: "That's bull! PT Boats are used as landing craft because they are *dependable*, something Army guys don't understand. Dropping you guys off is the easy part. When the troops need help on the beach, the Navy PT boats stay right there and provide cover! Army landing craft pulls up its landing ramp and retreats like a dog. Runs away from a fight with its tail between its legs!"

If a fistfight was not already in progress by this time, it soon would be until military police arrived on the scene. I can't say that I ever witnessed a bar fight since I didn't drink, but I have heard stories about them. My only real involvement in drinking as a pass time was when I regularly sold my monthly beer allotment to the highest bidder, usually as late in the month as possible, to get the best price.

We got to be so useful during beach landings that the enemy began to attack PT bases all over the South Pacific. I'll never forget my first experience with one of their attacks. I was up early, walking (and probably praying) in the light of the early Pacific sunrise. Our PT boats were docked along two parallel boardwalks that jutted out into the bay. The boats were lined up three deep at each dock position, all three tied together, with only the boat closest to the boardwalk being tied to the dock on a short line.

I had no idea that Japanese warplanes were also out that same morning, coming straight toward our base with the sun to their backs. I didn't see them until they banked and began to line up to strafe and bomb our base. I could see that they were going to start with our PT boats all lined up in rows along the dock. What happened next is like remembering a dream that happened long, long ago.

I remember yelling an alert and then running toward PT-81. All I could think of was getting her and as many other boats as possible out of the way of the approaching attack. As I ran down the boardwalk, I reached down and threw anchor line after anchor line into the water. The first plane was now lined up parallel with the boats. And I was running out of time.

PT-81 was tied next to the dock just ahead of me when the Japanese fighter began to spray the area with live ammunition. I could see the wood splinters exploding up and out of the boat decks and hear the ping of bullets ricocheting off torpedoes and the metal depth-charge canisters. The enemy plane screamed past me less than 100 feet away, rose up, and banked into a sharp turn. I threw PT-81's anchor line into the water. The line was purposely cut short enough so that it wouldn't get tangled up in the prop, just in case you had to leave in a hurry and let it drag in the water in an emergency. And I definitely had created an emergency for myself.

I wondered at that moment what the Japanese pilot was thinking. He had seen me and was probably trying to decide if he should use his next pass to pick off a young boatman who dared challenge him or if he should spray a long line of boats with live ammunition.

He was already well into his turn for his return flight. I reached into PT-81 and fired up my faithful engines. They started at the touch of the ignition switch and pushed the two PT boats tied to PT-81 out and away from the dock. By this time, the base was alive and bristling with return fire from every direction.

In a matter of seconds, the Japanese plane was lined up with the second boardwalk. PT-81 faithfully towed the other two boats out into the bay as the Japanese pilot evidently decided that destroying boats was more productive for his mission than chasing after me.

A fair amount of assets were spared by my efforts that day. And I was recommended for a personal Presidential Citation. Our commander later approached me with a request for my approval to have it issued as a unit Presidential Citation instead to demonstrate appreciation to the entire PT unit, something to which I readily agreed. Our unit was lined up and proudly received the award.

Chapter 19

KAMIKAZE - Port BOW

The tide of war had been in favor of Japan until the Battle of Lyte, where the U.S. won a major victory and severely crippled the Japanese Navy Fleet. Both the U.S. and the Japanese knew that Lyte was a key to the Philippines and to accessing the Japanese mainland. Each threw everything they had into the battle, and the U.S. won. History would reveal that even the Japanese emperor was heard to say that the loss of Lyte made the Japanese mainland vulnerable to U.S. occupation.

In a desperate attempt to regain the upper hand, Japan turned to the use of Kamikaze, or suicide, aircraft. The literal translation of the word "Kamikaze" roughly translates into English as "Divine Wind." Divine Wind refers to violent typhoons in the history of Japan that had protected their homeland from invading Mongolian ships sailing down from the north, first in the year 1274 and again in 1281.

Kamikaze pilots were typically very young men trained in Saki-laced rituals to believe that they, too, were like the Divine Winds . . . once again divinely called to protect their homeland from foreign invasion. The Kamikaze planes were Japanese fighter planes stripped of their weapons and armament. They were refitted with extra fuel tanks, explosives to ignite the fuel on impact, and sometimes torpedoes. The whole thing was a rigging for a one-way trip into battle.

Our first encounter with the Kamikaze was in the Battle of Minoros, directly after the U.S. Victory at Lyte. The Pacific sky was literally full of over 40 Kamikaze suicide planes that arrived at the battle scene and literally hurled themselves at U.S. targets. Japanese Kamikaze fell out of the sky like rain.

One of the nightmares that have been a part of my life since the end of WW II involves the Kamikaze. This nightmare scene typically opens with a firefight between Japanese fighter planes and PT-81. As the rest of my crewmen continue the battle with fighters, my dream attention is drawn to search the sky for other dangers that I can feel are coming even before I know what they are.

Let's look at this recurring dream of the Kamikaze in greater detail. I am searching the sky and suddenly become alert. I feel something I cannot hear. I hear something I cannot see.

I spot something in the distance. Sometimes, it is a group of planes; this time, I only see one. I am the first one to see him. I watch and then recognize the outline of a Japanese fighter. I stare. The plane is slow, almost laboring to stay in the air. He's flying sluggishly because he's overloaded.

I yell to the others, "KAMIKAZE . . . PORT bow."

My fingers lock my hands onto my Oldsmobile M4 37 mm cannon as I prepare to pump round after round into the approaching plane. I am tense and suddenly interrupted by the thought of the pilot in that plane. He is a man, a young man, like myself. The thought lasts but an instant. The "man" in that plane is intent on dying today and on taking me and as many others as he can with him. I force myself, almost angrily, to focus on the plane.

Everyone has abandoned all other targets. They swing their guns around to track and fire upon the Japanese suicide pilot, now arching in a long dive toward us. I can see him. He's lining us up in his sights. If there had been several, we would have each called out our target. I can even hear their cries and know them by their voices. "I've got 9 o'clock!" "12 o'clock is mine!" "3 o'clock is mine . . . he's aaall mine."

But there is only one this time. And he's going to get everything we've got.

The enemy plane is packed full of explosives and, perhaps, torpedoes. His guns have been removed and replaced with extra fuel tanks that will spray liquid fire on impact. He knows he's on a one-way trip. He wants to die. He has been chosen and convinced that, in the battle for the safety of his homeland, an "honorable death" is more desirable than his life. After pre-flight training and a ceremony of Ritual and Saki, he feels that he flies like the Divine Wind . . . like the homeland-saving storms of old.

Meanwhile, *I've* got only *one* thought. I'm riveted on that plane. It's him or me. Time seems to have slowed, but we'll know here shortly. It will be over in real-time, the time it will take you to read the next ten lines of type.

We are all concentrating on dropping him. We're throwing everything we have at him. He doesn't even have to hit us to put us under. All he has to do is survive long enough to hit the water and explode close enough to us to spray us with shrapnel and burning explosives.

My 37 mm M4 is built to cushion my arms and body from the hammering explosion of 2 shells a second, but my arms are tense, and my body vibrates to the sound of the gun as the Kamikaze approaches. A thought pierces its way through everything.

"Will I ever get used to this?" My answer comes almost as an audible reply. "O, God. I *hope* not."

I can hear the whine of the Kamikaze engine as he closes in. Engine oil streams toward the tail of the plane as his engine freezes up. The plane becomes a dead steel missile, full of explosives, on a trajectory toward our boat.

Our skipper has been racing ahead of the plane on purpose and suddenly darts into a 90-degree turn. He jams the throttles full forward. The engines are one of my responsibilities, and I strain to hear their response. They respond instantly with a deep-throated roar. The boat banks sharply and darts away seconds before the Kamikaze hits the water. Those are valuable seconds. My engines buy us the time we need. The difference is between life and death.

A massive explosion erupts behind us, just beyond the point where the skipper turned. We're just outside the imaginary circle that would have included us in a deadly spray of shrapnel and burning fuel. Liquid fire, explosions, and shrapnel are now traveling in what had been the direction of the plane, toward the very spot in the water where we had been just seconds ago. I'm already spinning my 37 mm cannon in search of other targets and to catch a glimpse of shrapnel from the Kamikaze plane spinning out of the air. Some of it is deflected toward us and hitting the water close behind. It disappears into the churning wake of our speeding PT boat.

My tense body is suddenly overcome with exhaustion and sinks rearward against the gun straps. And then, suddenly...

My head hits the mattress of our bed. 1 am sweating. The lights are on, and I immediately lurch forward, awake. I look around and catch sight of my wife, who is coming toward me . . . as she has so many times before. She reaches out and holds me now as I cry uncontrollably in her arms . . . longer and more intensely now than I ever have before. It has been this way ever since I started writing my book.

All of this is an intense and terrible experience. My writer heard me record this during one of our sessions. He's concerned and checks more and more regularly now with family members about slowing down or pulling back for a while . . . about getting counseling.

I have talked to my wife and my sons and daughters. We have prayed alone and together . . . and we all agree that we need to continue.

When I tell these stories, even the ones that are not about the dreams, I find myself hesitant. I search for words to express what I remember, what I feel, and what I sometimes almost see. When I hear the final text read back to me (since I cannot see to read) and find that it does express what I was trying to say, I get emotional.

It is such a relief to realize that someone has finally heard what I have been feeling. I am going to continue. I have no doubt that if I do all I can, the Lord will do the rest. I do wish, however, that it wouldn't take so long.

I am amazed that my writer has understood me as I have thrashed and struggled to find ways to be heard. When asked about this, he smiled at first and told me that his methods of listening to me were a big secret. My body language, the tone of my voice, the hesitations, my head turning from side to side to search the four corners of the living room ceiling for Kamikaze, and my clenched fists rising up to trigger height all add color to what I say. He didn't want to call attention to any of that at first because he didn't want to make me self-conscious so that I would ruin his extra source of information. He and I have gotten along great this way since the day we met in October 2011.

Chapter 20

The Evening of the Just-in-Case Notes to Our Mothers

PT-81 was part of a large number of squadrons that went on patrol almost every night for months at a time as the war intensified. We typically left our base before 2400 hours. That's 12:00 midnight for those of you who need a translation. We would get back to base at about 6:00 AM, then divide our time between maintaining the boat, maintaining ourselves, getting some sleep, and being briefed on our assignment for the next night. The few hours before leaving on the night patrol were typically ours to sleep, to relax, or sometimes just to talk.

Johnson and I were sitting quietly on board PT-81 one evening, talking now and then but mostly just relaxing as best we could while waiting for the upcoming night patrol. It wasn't unusual for the two of us to end up together, not only because neither of us was into drinking or serious partying but also because of a bond that we had as part of a small, special group of four PT crewmen. Johnson and I and two others were the only remaining survivors in a group of nearly 300 PT crewmen in RON-13 that had started out together in the Aleutian Islands.

Our survival rate, however, was not our topic that evening, at least not in the beginning.

It was a beautiful South Pacific evening. A quiet blanket of darkness covered the signs of war that were all around us. Palm trees stood silhouetted against the evening sky. The ocean made a gentle sound as it lapped against the dock. Even the dark outline of the PT boats around us seemed to somehow fit into the sights and sounds of a quiet Pacific evening. They looked a little like a fishing fleet there, in the dark.

After one particularly long interval of quiet reflection, Johnson's voice came out of the darkness.

"Hey, Milt, will you write your mom's name and address on this piece of paper for me?"

I was surprised at his question and startled by what I sensed was coming next. I took the paper, wrote the information, and handed it back. As he took the paper, he handed me a folded paper with his mother's name and address written carefully on the otherwise blank page. His next words hung in the air for a few moments before I could answer.

"Milt . . . will you go see my mother, just in case something happens to me, and deliver a message? And I'll do the same for you."

I sat there for what seemed like too long, then answered. "Sure, Johnson. What's the message."

"Tell her how much I have loved her my whole life. Tell her how precious she is in my memories of her and that I have taken those memories with me to wherever I am now. Tell her it's okay for her to be sad and okay to miss me for a little while but that I know I will be with her again someday. As far as what happened to me out here, tell her not to be concerned about it. Tell her that I was doing what I knew the Lord wanted me to do."

"And Milt . . . could you give her one last big hug for me?"

I eventually managed to say, "OK," but could not say any more than that for some time. Before we left on patrol that night, I would tell him, "That's just what I had in mind for you to tell my mom, Johnson. You tell her the very same thing from me." I thanked him, and we shook hands.

We then busied ourselves with sorting through the cases of ammunition assigned to our gun to be sure it was clean, dry, and lubricated. We did that every night before leaving so that it wouldn't jam during a firefight in whatever might be coming up that night. It was Johnson's turn to feed the ammo that night that would be behind the 37 mm. I'd be firing.

Just before 2400 hrs. that night, Skipper threw the throttle forward, and 3600 horsepower lifted PT-81 up and out of the water, leaving waves behind us that rocked and bumped the other PT boats against the dock. The crews still on the dock yelled something and waved their fists at us. We waved back as if we thought they were saying goodbye.

Johnson was killed the next day.

Chapter 21

The Sky Full of Steel, Glass, and Whatever it Takes to Build a Ship

The performance of the PT boats and their crews became legendary in the eyes of both the enemy we fought and the fighting men we served. Our reputation did not come, however, without a price. Not many know that PT crew survival rates were the lowest in the U. S. Military. In many cases, those of us who survived carried our injuries in our bodies, hearts, and minds for the rest of our lives.

PT patrols were originally on nighttime duty. But, as the war escalated with the use of Kamikaze aircraft and more frequent Japanese air raids, we ended up being on call 24 hours a day. On 4 Jan 1945, we were on daytime patrol when we received a radio message from a U.S. supply ship requesting assistance.

The ship was carrying a crew of 71 merchant marines and a cargo hold full of supplies and live ammunition in an area that had seen an increased use of Kamikaze aircraft. We all knew that it was highly likely that a Japanese suicide plane was either already on the scene or soon would be. Our radio lit up again, and we received the welcome news that PT-78 had also heard the distress call and was on its way.

Minutes later, we arrived on the scene to find Japanese fighters strafing the supply ship and a Japanese Kamikaze in the distance laboring its way toward the battle scene. The Kamikaze was overloaded with high explosives in place of guns. Extra fuel tanks were awkwardly strapped to the plane, transforming it into a highly effective, human-delivered suicide bomb.

Both PT boats banked sharply and raced to meet the incoming Japanese Kamikaze in an effort to drop it into the ocean before it could reach the U.S. supply ship. The full force of the firepower on two PT boats sent overlapping streams of ammunition and tracers arcing up into the oncoming suicide plane.

Our tracer bullets indicated that the plane was now flying through a steady hail of live ammunition. It was impossible to believe as we watched it just keep coming toward us without any indication of being hit. As the plane approached the point of flying over our position, Skipper maneuvered PT-81 to keep our guns in the best position for firing, which meant that we were moving closer to the supply ship. PT-78 was between our boat and the supply ships and in even more danger than we were if we could not stop that plane. As the Kamikaze passed overhead, I could see my tracer bullets actually passing right through the plane, and still, it did not falter.

We were all running out of time. The Kamikaze was just about to hit its target, and we were way too close to the supply ship. If it exploded, we would be in trouble.

The suicide plane faltered just 500 yards from its target as its engine froze, and a trail of fire streamed out behind the damaged plane. It continued on its path and hit the target midship, just above the water line. The plane exploded into a ball of fire that first flattened against the side of the ship and then sent fingers of fire reaching up and over its massive deck. Both PT boats roared to life and banked into sharp turns in an effort to take us away from what was going to happen next.

PT-78 was some distance behind us as we both raced away from the now-burning ship. Suddenly, the ship literally disappeared in a massive series of explosions and billowing clouds of smoke that tore it apart from stem to stern. PT-78 was completely engulfed in the fire and billowing smoke that reached half the distance between PT-81 and where the ship had been seconds before.

Two of us, myself on the rear gun and Johnson . . . who had been with me since our squadron had been transferred to the South Pacific, were both near the stern of PT-81, and we both knew that a blast of air was on its way.

We turned to dive for cover below deck but never made it. A blast of air from the explosions slammed into us at the speed of sound, over 700 MPH, and threw us to the deck. We lay there stunned and temporarily deafened as repeated concussions from the blasts, one for each of the series of explosions from the ammunition that had filled the cargo hold, pummeled us.

We lay motionless and then began to stir. We looked up to see the massive clouds of billowing smoke rising higher and higher above the now-empty space where the supply ship had been. This wasn't the first ship full of ammunition, supplies, and Soldiers that we had seen explode and then literally disappear in a billowing cloud of smoke that rose into the blue

South Pacific sky. Some were ships with Japanese markings. Others had markings of our own.

This was, however, the first ship that found us this far within the circle of death that would soon rain down on us from the sky. We were in big, big trouble. Shrapnel was still rising higher and higher, but it would soon be arcing out in all directions in a rain of steel, glass, and whatever else it takes to build a ship.

Chapter 22

Shrapnel Soaring like Steel Kites in the Sky

The concussion from the explosion that raced over us had actually lifted our boat out of the water and slammed us back down with a force that left us momentarily deaf and stunned. As Johnson and I stirred and began to recover, we knew what was coming next. I noticed that it was strangely quiet.

My ears rang as my hearing returned. Then, I began to recognize the water splashes in the distance that were moving closer to our boat as pieces of shrapnel began raining out of the sky. Johnson and I each scrambled for as much cover as we could find, which wasn't much. I ended up at first huddled next to my gun turret and then decided the barrel of my M4 would provide better protection and be more likely to deflect shrapnel that would be hitting us within seconds.

I ended up on my back . . . looking up. Everything seemed to move in slow motion. I could see large pieces of steel soaring in the Pacific breeze like steel kites in the sky. They spun and twisted on their way from high in the sky down toward the water . . . and toward our boat. My attention was pulled to one piece of shrapnel, high in the air, that at first spun away but then seemed to spin and drift slowly back toward us until it was directly overhead.

I remember thinking about what would happen if those large pieces hit our boat.

I tried to move and realized that I was paralyzed. I hadn't been hit, but I couldn't move. I can't explain it even today. I couldn't even speak. I lay on my back, counting on my gun barrel to deflect larger pieces of debris. But one piece of steel was now directly overhead. Its shape is burned into my memory: a 4-sided piece, shaped like a knife blade, about 2 feet long, 2 inches wide at one end, 6 inches at the other.

I again strained to move or to cry out, but nothing happened. Split seconds and slow motion seemed to speed up and rush forward as it caught up to the normal rush and blur of time. The one piece that I had been watching now spiraled rapidly toward where I lay. I strained with all the strength in my mind and body to the point that I finally heard my voice groan in a faint Heavenward cry for help. My body became rigid, like a compressed spring, before it was released. And then a sudden violent spasm tore through me, spreading my arms and legs wide. There was one last flash of that same piece of steel, and then there was the deafening clatter of steel pieces falling all around. Sounds of splitting wood came like cries from our PT boat as steel sliced and tore into her wooden deck and into everything else around me.

I heard Johnson cry, "*Milt . . . I've been HIT!*" And then it was over.

I opened my eyes. Shrapnel was everywhere. Johnson was stretched out nearby with a piece of shrapnel sliced into his helmet. I could tell by looking at him that he was dead, just hours after our final exchange of notes to our mothers.

I untangled myself from the debris and sat up to find my blood-soaked trousers ripped open from top to bottom along both inseams. There was no pain. I was suspicious and cautiously reached for my legs. I ran my hand up one leg and down the other and was relieved to find everything intact. The inside of my left leg was bruised from my inner thigh above my knee down to my ankle. My right inner leg had been sliced open from top to bottom.

To this day, I can't explain what happened that first tightened my body and then threw it into a spasm and into a position that saved my life. The final damage report showed a hole in the deck between where my legs had been frozen together until the seizure or spasm threw them apart. The 26-inch steel shrapnel knife that I had watched sailing in slow motion would have severed my legs from my body. I haven't spoken of it before. I can hardly do so now.

There were two in our crew that could move around, and they helped those that couldn't. They wrapped my leg in bandages, and I became one of those who could attend the others. One of our engines was still idling. Two were destroyed by shrapnel that had pierced the deck. Only one man in our crew wasn't injured. Johnson was dead. The skipper had a broken back.

You did what needed to be done, or you died. We arranged those who were seriously hurt below deck. We didn't have cots or mattresses; the injured were made as comfortable as possible on the wooden planks below. The less seriously hurt were placed in rows on the deck.

We radioed a May Day and knew that help was on the way.

Chapter 23

An Empty Pail Floating in a Quiet South Pacific Sea

The previous chapter described what happened when we could not bring down the Kamikaze that hit one of our supply ships. Both the Kamikaze and the ship disappeared in a series of explosions. The Japanese fighters that had accompanied the Kamikaze were gone . . . all shot down.

The time after a battle can be a dramatic contrast compared to what has just happened if you have the time or capability left to notice. The supply ship had literally vanished in a shutter of repeated explosions. You might expect to see at least some floating, smoking, burning debris. Yet, I remember looking back and marveling at how quickly the South Pacific battle area repaired itself and returned to its serene, blue water self as if nothing had happened.

The signs that a ship had ever been there were few. The only evidence to bear witness to the existence of a huge ship occupied by 71 souls was one upside-down pail floating calmly in the blue Pacific water, shrapnel scattered on the decks of the two PT boats, and one unconscious U.S. Sailor floating face up with a life jacket that held his head above water and saved his life.

The three of us who could still get around on PT-81 pulled the one surviving sailor aboard, attended to the casualties on our boat, and then turned our attention to our badly damaged companion boat, PT-78.

Our engines were damaged to the point that only one could operate at idle speed. We slowly made our way over to the crippled PT-78 and loaded their injured crewmen onto our boat. There were two PT-78 crewmen who were not hurt, and they chose to stay with their boat to help hook it up for towing when help arrived.

The trip took us an hour, considerably longer than any previous trip home, when our 3600 HP had driven us up on top of the water at 42 mph. We pulled into the dock, unloaded our casualties, and moved PT-81 out of the way to an area reserved for boats damaged beyond repair.

PT-81, our home away from home, remained docked until the end of the war. She was then stripped of all metal parts and burned along with hundreds of other PT boats, ranging in condition from beyond repair to almost good as new but too expensive to keep around.

The incident report described the damage to the boat, listed the casualties, and recorded the timeline as follows:

1705 - On Station

1708 - Air raid alert. Went to general quarters.

1712 - Sustained combat damage resulting in several holes in the deck planking . . . followed by a list of casualties to personnel.

All this translates to meaning that PT-81 responded to the request for assistance in 3 minutes and then engaged in a battle that lasted 4 minutes.

Nature heals itself when possible, doing its best to cover damaged areas that are scarred beyond repair. The sea, sky, and air ravaged by the hand of war mended within minutes, at least in the eyes and ears of those in the battle zones. On land, war-torn beaches, jungles, fields, and meadows gaped like open wounds and then softened with overgrowth in the weeks, months, and seasons that followed.

And so, it seems to also be with war damage inflicted upon fighting men and women, as well as upon the innocent who are caught in the middle. There is no such thing as a good war. War is a terrible thing, and, as with nature, the wounds of men are healed where possible and covered over where they are found to be scarred beyond repair.

Chapter 24

From the End of PT-81 to the End of the WW II

The previous chapter left you with a fatally crippled PT-81 that had slowly made its way back to base with a cargo of casualties. The crews of both PT-81 and PT-78 had paid the price for not being able to bring down a Japanese Kamikaze before it hit a U.S. supply ship loaded with ammunition.

This chapter and the two following are being added after I had previously decided that the book was complete.

I really did think that I was done. After all, I had documented the service life of PT-81 and had described the trauma of its final battle. We had left the boat where I last saw it docked back at a Pacific Island base damaged beyond repair and waiting for demolition.

My original "end-of-book" decision didn't stand up in the face of what happened in the next few days. I had a dream that differed entirely from any of the nightmares I had previously experienced. The dream was non-violent. It was a meeting with my WW II best friend, H.W. Johnson, that made it very clear to me that this book was NOT finished.

Among other things, I came out of that dream startled to realize that the book was not really about PT-81 but about a man named Milton Rackham. And, for that story to be told, we need to go a little further.

The war was over for PT-81, but for the survivors, World War II continued to rage on with increasing ferocity. Crew members with minor injuries were treated at base camp and received new boat assignments immediately. I was transferred, along with four other more seriously wounded crew members, to a base hospital much like the MASH units you see on TV.

I was in the hospital for just two weeks and then released early to help meet the increasing demand for PT crewmen. I was discharged and assigned to serve under the watchful eye of my new skipper on PT-155. I arrived along with a suitcase full of bandages, medications, and antiseptics so I could continue treating my slowly-healing injuries right there in the field of battle.

I had also picked up a case of Jungle Rot (or Trench Foot) while I was in the hospital. A military field hospital was not the healthiest place to be. If you did not have Malaria or

Jungle Rot or some other common tropical disease when you went into a base hospital, you could almost be sure you'd have one or more of these diseases if you did make it out the door alive.

I was eager to get back out on the boat. My eagerness had nothing to do with bravery, a macho attitude, or anything else like that. We all knew that the tide of war had changed in our favor and that the final push to end the war and get back home would require everything we had to get the job done. The enemy had already demonstrated their suicidal belief that death in defense of their homeland was more honorable than surrender. So, once I left the hospital, I was put immediately back on night-time patrols and daytime air raid detail.

In June and July of 1945, U.S. military planners were already well into the final preparations for a conventional invasion of the Japanese homeland. At this point, the American war machine back in the States had been in full operation for several years. Freshly shipped equipment, ammunition, and supplies began to accumulate in amounts across the Pacific that were beyond imagination.

A U.S. bomber pilot relayed his observation that, while flying at 5,000 feet over the U.S. Navy invasion forces gathered in the Pacific Ocean, he could see a vast array of U.S. ships, carriers, boats, and watercraft of every kind extended in every direction beyond the horizon, as far as the eye could see.

All of this escalation meant that our PT boat patrols continued without slowing right up until war operations ceased just hours after the dropping of the first atomic bomb on 6 August 1945. I know that there is a lot of controversy about the use of the atomic bomb. As one who was on the front lines, however, I can say with certainty that the decision to use it was the correct one. In exchange for the sacrifice of two Japanese cities and a total casualty count of 250,000 souls, literally *millions* of lives were saved.

In my case, my slow-healing wounds continued to be a problem during my continued PT boat service, and my skipper had me transferred back to the hospital for ongoing treatment just prior to the end of the war. My condition remained unchanged for days and then came the two red lines—blood poisoning. There was one traveling up my injured right leg and another one going up my injured left arm. After one early evening examination, I heard the two doctors discussing my case as they stood just outside the area where I lay. They talked about amputation when the red lines reached my elbow and my knee. The medic came in with more intensive levels of treatment and medication and left.

I remember that night as one of the darkest, loneliest, most frightening nights of my life. I filled the first few hours with prayerful cries of sorrow for my situation and a pleading for either recovery or an end to it all. I questioned my Heavenly Father about why I had been spared time and time again if my life was to be one of pain and nightmares and now the loss of limbs.

As the hours of that night wore on, my prayers turned to a plea for understanding and discernment as to *why* I was being spared while so many around me were being killed. Now, I was myself, one who was trained to kill. And kill I did. And yet I lived on, becoming ever less worthy of living because I killed *again* and *again* and *again*.

I pled for the strength to believe that I was fighting for more than just my own self-preservation, simply so I could continue killing. I desperately needed to believe that I was fighting to protect my country, my family, and my future children.

As the final hours of a long and anguished night came to a close, my prayers shifted to a plea that I could be released from the hospital...*with* my limbs intact.

My faith was being tested and tried in ways that may well be understandable only to other veterans who have experienced similar circumstances. And there are those who have faced war-time experiences that are far worse than anything I had to face.

As I awoke in the early light of the next day from what ended up being a short, fitful night's sleep, I yearned to feel *worthy*. Worthy of the love, mercy, and gift of the atonement provided by my Savior. It was something I would eventually regain in the years ahead at the hands of one of the Lord's called servants, a good bishop in my hometown.

The next morning the red lines were found to be retreating. Within days, my condition improved, and I asked my doctors when I would be going home. They looked at each other, then at me, and asked if I thought I was ready to go home. I nodded yes, and soon after that, I was on a ship with hundreds of others on a six-week trip to San Francisco.

Chapter 25

My Plan to Spend the Rest of My Life as a Hermit

The trip home was not the happy occasion you might think it would have been. Several events that happened during those six weeks added several new items to my list of material for future nightmare topics.

The trip to the ship's mess hall took us past a row of locked, heavy metal doors. These rooms contained the shells of servicemen who were mentally shattered by their wartime experiences. We could hear them screaming, yelling, and wailing uncontrollably. Sometimes, they would peer at us with empty eyes through a small view-hole in their doors. Some were in straight jackets. Others were strapped to chairs. Or to their beds. The cramped space below the deck had always made me feel uneasy. But walking past those rooms six times a day to and from the mess hall for the six weeks I spent on that ship was more than I could stand. War had taken its toll on the men in those rooms, and they were experiencing a never-ending hell on earth.

I was physically leaving the war zone behind me, but the nightmares that I would experience for the next 66 years were already well underway. The sight, sound, and emotion of those men locked behind those heavy metal doors became a regular part of my nighttime visitations. And the only thought there to greet me when I woke was, *"There, but for the grace of God, go I."*

I was filled with such fear and dread that I ended up having to find an alternate route to the mess hall that took me on a long, meandering path that could have been the length of the huge ship for all I knew. But *anything* was better than going past those poor souls day after day.

We docked at San Francisco after stopping all over the South Pacific to pick up veterans on their way home. Soon after landing, I headed for home and arrived in the welcoming arms of my mother.

My mother began to ask me right away if I was okay, and I would assure her that all was well. But I knew better, and so did she. I was far from being okay. The sounds of my nightmares would awaken her in the night, and my biggest fear became that I might harm her when she rushed to my room to try and comfort me. I tried to explain to her why she should stay away, but I don't recall that she ever understood.

Although I was relieved to be home, I was also absolutely convinced that I could not be part of normal society. I knew that I was far too dangerous to be with. Looking back, it was as if I had decided that the world and I would be better off if I became some kind of hermit for the preservation of all concerned.

What I had done in the way of repeated killings was so terrible, so unforgivable, that it would be best shut away forever. After all, the war was over, America was at peace, times were improving, and people, including most veterans, were moving on. Yet all I had to offer was one long tale of misery.

I didn't know how to contribute to society, and I didn't know how to talk about the war. As far as I was concerned, anything that I had to say would come across as being either someone looking for sympathy or, worse yet, as some glory seeker who was seeking a pat on the back for having lived through it all. Even now, as I see my thoughts and words in writing, I am concerned that there are readers who might be offended by my story, but I have made the difficult decision that I must go on.

I have been able to open up to my friend, who is writing this beyond anything I have ever been able to do before in my effort to expose my nightmares to the light of day. There are things here that even my family has never heard before. I just hope and pray that these writings will tip the scales toward a better understanding rather than disdain for me and for what I had to do.

After a few months of hanging around home, just eating, sleeping, sitting, and staring into space, I finally found a job to sustain myself. It was a stand-alone job at a sawmill grading the quality of the finished lumber. It was just what I thought I needed. It was so noisy that I was isolated from everyone else and didn't have to talk to anyone any more than necessary.

Things happened, however, that reinforced my resolve to retreat from others. In one case, a group of playful co-workers decided to initiate an innocent new hire. They sent him to sneak up behind me with a piece of steel, with the instructions that he was to drop it behind me to "see Milt jump."

The sound of the dropping sheet of steel hit me like an explosion. The attack reaction it triggered was over before I even knew what I had done. My first awareness was one of finding myself standing in a crouched position off to one side, trying to figure out what had happened and what was going to happen next. The poor young fellow on the floor was carried away with a broken jaw. And I was devastated. Not only had I hurt an innocent person, but this and other experiences like it were adding to a growing body of evidence pointing to one conclusion: that I did not belong anywhere in society.

I did not attend church for the first year I was home. After that, I began to occasionally when my mother would ask for help with something. But even then, I did not feel worthy enough to sit through a complete service.

I ended up getting to know the bishop, and before long, he began to call me during the week to help him with various tasks. We would drive places to help a soul in need now and then, and he would often ask me how things were going. I always answered, "Fine, just fine." I would then make light conversation to distract him from how I was really doing.

Eventually, he began to ask me what was bothering me, and I changed my response to a casual "Nothing. Nothing is bothering me." I would then try to go into some improved level of conversation since I could see that I was not being successful in distracting him from the fact that I was "bothered" inside.

One day, after one too many of my responses of "nothing," he pulled into a parking lot, stopped the car, and turned off the engine.

"Guess what, Milt," He began. "How about if you and I sit here and talk about this topic called 'nothing' for a while? Would you like to open our time here together with a prayer?"

Without covering a lot of detail, I can tell you that the weeks and months that followed with this good bishop did, indeed, get me to the point where I was able to resolve my yearning to feel worthy. I found the cleansing I had sought since that night in the military hospital through the love and atoning sacrifice of my Savior, Jesus Christ.

I found that I was able to attend church from that point on. But I still felt that, forgiven or not, I remained a certifiable danger to others. For this reason, I fully intended to stay clear of the rest of society as much as possible for the remainder of my life.

Two years after having returned home from the War, I ended up at a church activity that included families I had known before I left for the war eight years earlier. There was a young lady named Carol in one of the families that had grown up to be a beautiful young woman while I was gone. She was easy to talk to, and I mustered the courage to ask her to dance. I was really impressed with her, and as the evening wore on, I ended up asking her if I could escort her home.

Her answer was that I would have to ask her dad about something as important as that. I knew her dad from way back, and before I could talk to him, he came over and struck up a conversation.

To make a long story short, I began dating Carol Johnson, and as time went by, she ended up messing up my plans to be a hermit. We began talking about getting married. I gave her a chance to have second thoughts by warning her about my WW II nightmares and then held my breath. She listened to what I had to say and announced that she could handle it. She helped me make some corrections in my direction in life, and we were married on the 26th of May, 1950. We now have three sons, Rodney, Aaron, and Kevin, and four daughters, Nan, Glenda, Rosanne, and Cindy.

Now that I have acknowledged in writing that my sweetheart, Carol, helped me make some 'corrections in my directions,' I am beginning to realize something that is perhaps the most important part of this book *that my life's journey is about a bigger picture than just the problems I have faced.*

And I believe all of us can benefit from remembering that.

Chapter 30

A New Kind of Night-time Dream

If you have been able to stick with me through all of this, you are aware that these last few chapters are the result of having a PT-81 dream that differed from my PTSD nightmares. This dream occurred immediately after I had prematurely declared an end to this book.

The next morning after the dream, I eagerly called my friend in Big Rapids, who is writing this for me, to tell him what happened. He answered the phone. What I poured out probably sounded like one long sentence:

"Guess what happened last night, I had a dream about Johnson, a different kind of dream . . . Not a nightmare . . . All I can remember about the dream is when I woke up; it felt like I had been with Johnson. He talked about my book. He asked me if it was done . . . and now I'm not sure . . . What do you think?"

I took a deep breath and listened. There was silence at the Big Rapids end of the line, and then he said, "Sooo . . . what do you want to do about it?"

I asked him if we could reopen the book. We rearranged our calendars and began recording additions to the book, including several of the previous chapters and the following description of the dream.

I awoke from the dream with an intense awareness that I had just returned from a meeting with my WW II buddy, H.W. Johnson. As I woke up and tried to capture the details, the dream began rapidly fading. Perhaps you have experienced something similar in your own dream history.

The Johnson meeting in the dream felt like the many meetings we had almost every evening in the hours prior to leaving on our night-time patrols. Even though the details of the dream have dimmed, I am going to try to create the feeling of what happened based on my memory of Johnson and the time we spent together when he was alive.

Johnson was the same as he always was. We were glad to see each other. It was a warm, pleasant experience, a welcome change from my usual PTSD nightmares. I looked around, expecting to see the others, but it was just the two of us.

The last time we met was 66 years ago. We had exchanged contact information for our mothers, just in case something happened to one of us. I wanted to talk to him about my meeting with his sweet mother, but he didn't ask about that. It was as if he already knew, as if he had somehow been there.

It soon became obvious that Johnson wanted to talk about something else. He got right down to business in his typical, friendly manner.

"Hey, Milt...your book... is it done?"

"Yup, yup. Finished it this week."

"That's interesting. How come you left our names out of your book, Milt? Are you ashamed of us?"

His question startled me. I scrambled to insist that no, I was in no way ashamed of ANY of them.

"Aw," Johnson grinned as he dipped one toe into the warm Pacific water. "You're right, Milt. We really do know that you aren't ashamed of us. But, me and the guys, we wanted to get your attention, Milt. Did it work?"

He paused and looked directly at me. "You need to know that your book is not finished, Milt."

Johnson just sat there with a friendly smile. I couldn't answer out loud, but I nodded yes.

I felt myself getting uneasy. I understood where Johnson was going with all of this about having left something out of the book, about making the decision that it was done.

Neither one of us said anything for a little while. Johnson looked at me in his quiet, friendly way, letting me know that he understood what I was feeling inside.

Eventually, he asked me, "Are you going to finish your book?"

I paused to gain my composure so I would be able to do something besides nod my head. After a bit, I did nod, and I choked out the words, "Yes. Yes. I am going to finish my book, my book about Milt Rackham."

"Because I am not ashamed."

We were quiet for a while in the dream. Just like we used to be so many years ago on PT-81 while we were waiting to leave for one more night-time patrol.

The dream that night differed from any of the others in the past 66 years. I woke up and sat quietly. I was tense and felt like I was in a cold sweat, without the sweat, if that makes any sense.

Carol woke up and asked me if I was okay.

I said I was okay.

And I really meant it.

Epilogue

The Price of Liberty

I initially agreed to open up about my wartime experiences because a therapist told me it might help put an end to my suffering. Before closing it for good, I want to summarize a list of things that have come to light for me as a result of my having been able to follow through on that advice.

1. I have talked about feelings of "survivor guilt", about others being taken while I remained standing time and time again.
2. I recognized feelings of guilt for having become a trained killer of an uncounted number of men. I could not comprehend why I was being spared from becoming ever more unworthy by being allowed to kill again and again when God could have spared my worthiness by taking me home instead.
3. I recognized that *I* had judged *myself* as being unworthy of the gift of the atoning sacrifice of my Savior. The truth was that that decision was up to Him and not me.

4. I am hopeful that my new, non-violent dream may be a turning point for me in being able to put my nightmares to rest.
5. And finally, I have become increasingly aware of the current threats against our country and the need to stand and defend her one more time. Raising public awareness about the sacrifices made to preserve America matters more to me now than shielding myself from the discomfort I feel when I share my experiences.

Since finishing my book, my writer and I have traveled as often as my health will permit. We have talked about my book and my experiences with a growing number of people. Some have reached out to me after reading my book, and we've had the chance to discuss their own experiences and thoughts.

I was pleasantly surprised to receive a phone call from one veteran who read an early copy of this book. We talked at length about the price of liberty. We talked about those who stood up and protected our liberty with their lives and about wounded warriors whose lives have been changed forever because of their service. We discussed our own personal situations, the content of this book, and the impact it had on us.

We talked for hours over the course of many phone conversations as he reported his own progress in finding closure to his own PTSD nightmares. The following paragraph is based on the content of our many conversations.

"When I discovered Milt's book, I was both eager and apprehensive about reading it. Once I started, I couldn't put it down. I began to share Milt's WW II experience and contemplate my own service time.

Certain chapters were emotional for me and hard to read, not only because of what I was reading but also because I began to struggle with tears regarding my wartime experience. I am not an emotionally open person, and the tears and feelings I experienced were unusual and difficult for me. I was particularly moved by Milt's list at the end of his book, where he recognized his feelings of survivor guilt and unworthiness.

I read the book several times and decided I needed to take a hard look at my situation. There is a huge, old tree in our woods. It reminds me of a church or cathedral. It's one of my favorite places, a "safe place" to sit and think things through. Without getting into a lot of detail, suffice it to say I visited my tree, prayed about my PTSD nightmares, and quietly listened for answers. My thoughts turned to spiritual matters, forgiveness, and church attendance. I thought about the passage in Milt's book that says . . .

"There surely must be one person out there who needs to know they are not alone in trying to deal with war-time memories . . . or even non-war memories disrupting their life. May God bless both of us, you and me, whoever you are, that we will understand what the Lord would have us do."

Milt, I feel like I am one of those persons you mention in your book. I have not had a PTSD nightmare since my prayerful time under my tree as a result of having read your book. God bless you, man. It is my prayer that you, too, will find the relief you seek."

When I served in the U.S. Navy during World War II, I was fighting a war to protect my country, my family, and my future children and grandchildren. The veterans I know today feel the same- that we really *were* part of am elite group that laid everything on the line for our families and for the future of this country.

I find myself increasingly concerned, frustrated, and even frightened when I realize that current generations are losing track of the values that founded our nation. I am equally disturbed when I see that many seem unaware of the sacrifices we made to preserve it.

Americans are in danger. Terrible danger. We are losing the things that made this country the greatest in the world. This is a country whose values and principles became enriched by the cultures and traditions of those who came to be a part of it. We are a country that became a beacon to the rest of the world, a country that brought people from everywhere who were not only eager to come here but also to become a part of who we are.

And who are we? We are a people who yearn to be free. Free to work and keep the fruits of our labors, free to succeed and to prosper, free to learn from our failure and free to start again.

Above all, we are a people who yearn to be good, to be worthy. We are a people who yearn to improve ourselves and build a good world where everyone can have the same freedoms we enjoy.

We veterans stare in disbelief at reports of veteran funerals being picketed and disrupted. We are sickened by those who govern to enrich themselves in power and ill-gotten gains, who trade their votes for gain in secret and then, when exposed, publicly defend themselves with feigned outrage on televised newscasts and social media.

Where is the outrage when legislation opposed by the people is negotiated behind closed doors and passed anyway so we can "find out what it says"?

The good news to me is that veterans are not the only ones becoming aware of all of the above and more. The American people are awakening to the needs of the country, aware we are now dealing with issues far beyond party-line politics and party-line choices at the voting booth. We are now faced with choices between right and wrong, between good and evil.

Will we uphold the rule of law, or will we passively allow the ongoing erosion of our individual rights? Will we support candidates who commit to following the U.S. Constitution, or will we back those who aim to disregard it or interpret it out of existence altogether?

The federal government is expanding in size and power beyond anything originally defined in the U.S. Constitution, all at the expense of state, local, family, and individual sovereignty. Checks and balances in each of the three branches of the federal government have gone unused or, on the other end of the spectrum, have been horribly abused.

We must recognize that the ultimate check and balance rests with the people themselves. You and I. WE are entrusted with a sacred responsibility to be vigilant, to become informed, and to learn to measure all elected officials, candidates, issues, agendas, and proposed legislation against standards of measurement we trust.

My standards of measurement will be the Declaration of Independence, the U.S. Constitution, the Bill of Rights, the 10 Commandments, and personal prayer. I believe individuals, families, and states must retain the right to govern at the lowest possible level.

For me, my choice will be a constitutional Republic over any other form of government, constitutional adherence over interpretation, and the answers I receive to my prayers when I always inquire and then listen.

Thomas Jefferson warned at the time of the signing of the U.S. Constitution that *"The Price of Liberty is Eternal Vigilance."*

His warning is as true today as it was then. It is my prayer that an awakening has come in time to save the America paid for by the fathers and sons and the mothers and daughters who gave their lives or the lives of those they loved.

We are confronted by candidates, elected officials, issues, and agendas often hidden behind political party rhetoric, but the choices we must make are much more basic than that. It is time for Americans to meet on common ground, to come together, and finally focus our attention on saving the country.

The longer we wait to stand up for what this country was intended to be, the more difficult it will be to restore what is being taken away.

Appendix

PT-81 around the time of its commissioning in December 1942

Crewman on the U.S. PT Boat - 321 bring a Japanese survivor aboard at the battle of Surigao Strait

Milton Rackham, who passed away at home at the age of 98, is pictured here as a young Navy sailor during World War II (FoxNews.com)

Milt Rackham's Purple Heart

Above: US Campaign Victory and Services Medal. Right, Asiatic Pacific Campaign medal.

"You seep into him from behind with short bursts, watching your tracers. When the tracers are on target, you squeeze longer bursts."

Rackham, pictured here with his sons Rodney (left) and Aaron (right) reenacts his war-time role manning a gun turret after having resolved feelings of guilt through the writing of his book, "PT-81: Still On Nightmare Patrol" (FoxNews.com)

Milt Rackham and co-author, Myrl Thompson, May 2012 (The Daily News, Montcalm County, MI)

World War II veteran, Milton Rackham, is pictured here with his wife, Carol. (legacy.com)

World War II veteran, Milton Rackham, is pictured here with his wife, Carol. (legacy.com)

Milt Rackham with his sweetheart, Carol Johnson Rackham (legacy.com)

*We salute you one last time. Until we meet again, my friend.
Thank you for your service.*

Obituary

Private Milt Rackham passed away peacefully at home on the day after Memorial Day, 2023, at the age of 98. This is his family's tribute to him:

Milton Rackham, age 98, of Belding, Michigan, passed away Tuesday, May 30, 2023, at home. He was born April 23, 1925, in Bates, Idaho. He was a member of The Church of Jesus Christ of Latter-day Saints in Greenville, MI. He lived a good life; in his youth, he was a true cowboy herding cattle and sheep on the Wyoming range. At age 17, he entered the Navy during World War II as a PT crewman on PT-81. He served in the Aleutian Islands off the Alaskan Shores and later in the Pacific Islands. After his service, he worked as a construction worker on the Palisade Dam in Idaho. He met the love of his life, Carol Johnson, and was married on May 26, 1950, and celebrated 72 years before her passing. Later, he worked for Montgomery Wards as a sales manager for a number of years. He moved his family to Michigan, opened his upholstery business, and served the community of Belding for over 40 years. He loved fishing with or spending time with his grandchildren.

There never was a time that he ended a conversation with a friend or stranger that he didn't end with the phrase "Remember you're loved."

Milton and Carol had seven children, 32 grandchildren, 87 great-grandchildren, and ten great-great-grandchildren. Funeral services were held on Saturday, June 3, 2023, at The Church of Jesus Christ of Latter-day Saints. Services at the church concluded with a combined Military Service consisting of the VFW Post #4406 and American Legion Post #203 of Belding, MI.

Burial occurred in the Otisco Cemetery in Belding. Memorial contributions were made in Milton's name to The Church of Jesus Christ of Latter-day Saints for the benefit of their missionary program.

Author Bio

Myrl William Thompson grew up on his German immigrant grandparents' small farm in western Michigan in the 1940s. The time he spent on the farm taught him to love and respect veterans and old-timers by working alongside them and listening carefully to the stories they would tell. He learned to love all creatures, barnyard and otherwise, through the endless hours he spent playing and working among them.

A Master's graduate of Michigan State University's prestigious Kettering University (formerly the General Motors Institute), Mr. Thompson is an amateur author/illustrator and a retired engineer who worked in GM's Product Engineering and Design program for 45 years.

His first book, "*Skinny Little Frog*," was written for his own children in 1972 and set on the banks of his childhood farm. Other books he has written include Other books he has written include his own memoirs, entitled *Climbing Memory Mountain*, *The Dating Life of Mr. Clueless: Thoughts on Girls from the Old Swami*, *Santa Does the Six Step*, and *Emma: The Last 100 Years*. His daughter, Juli Anne Dalton, has also written her first children's book, entitled *Farm Song*.